94

THE
CHINESE-AMERICAN
HERITAGE

David M. Brownstone

Part of the America's Ethnic Heritage series
General Editors: David M. Brownstone and Irene M. Franck

Facts On File®

AN INFOBASE HOLDINGS COMPANY

The Chinese-American Heritage

Library of Congress Cataloging-in-Publication Data

Brownstone, David M.
    The Chinese-American heritage.
    (The America's ethnic heritage series)
    Bibliography: p.
    Includes index.
    1. Chinese Americans—History—Juvenile literature.
I. Title.   II. Series: America's ethnic heritage.
E184.C5B74   1988   973'.04951   88-10970
ISBN 0-8160-1627-5

British CIP data available on request

Printed in the United States of America

10 9 8 7 6 5 4 3 2

Contents

Preface

The Chinese-American Heritage is a volume in the *America's Ethnic Heritage* series, which explores the unique background of each of America's ethnic groups—their history and culture, their reasons for leaving home, their long journey to America, their waves of settlement in the new land, their often-difficult years of adjustment as they made their way into the American mainstream and their contributions to the overall society we call "America."

We would like to thank the many people who helped us in completing this work: our expert typists, Shirley Fenn and Mary Racette; Domenico Firmani, photo researcher *par excellence*; skilled cartographer Dale Adams; James Warren, our excellent editor at Facts On File; his very able assistants, Claire Johnston and Barbara Levine; publisher Edward Knappman, who supported the series from the start; and the many fine members of the Facts On File editorial and production staff.

We also express our special appreciation to the many librarians whose help has been indispensable in completing this work, especially to the incomparable staff of the Chappaqua Library—director Mark Hasskarl; the reference staff, including Mary Platt, Paula Peyraud, Terry Cullen, Martha Alcott, Carolyn Jones, and, formerly, Helen Barolini and Karen Baker; Jane McKean and Marcia Van Fleet and the whole circulation staff—and the many other librarians who, through the Interlibrary Loan network, have provided us with the research tools so vital to our work.

David M. Brownstone
Irene M. Franck

America's Ethnic Heritage

The United States is a great sea of peoples. All the races, nations, and beliefs of the world are met here. We live together, joined with each other while at the same time keeping our own separate identities. And it works. Sometimes there is pain and struggle for equality and justice, but it works—and will for as long as we all want it to.

We have brought with us to America all the ethnic heritages of the world. In that respect, there is no other place like this on earth—no other place where all the histories of all the peoples come together. Some have therefore called the United States a great "melting pot." But that is not quite right. We do not mix and completely merge our ethnic heritages. Instead we mix them, partially merge them, and at the same time keep important parts of them whole. The result is something unique called an American.

THE
CHINESE-AMERICAN
HERITAGE

1

The Chinese Heritage

This book is about the history of the Chinese who came to America. It is about the China they came from, the vastly different America they came to, and the Chinese-Americans they have become during the course of almost a century and a half in America. In a certain sense, it is also about the people Chinese-Americans are becoming, as all of us continue to mix and partially merge our personal and ethnic histories. America changes and we change with it, bringing all of our hopes, dreams, skills, qualities, and accomplishments with us. Like the people of all ethnic groups, Chinese-Americans bring their own history and special qualities with them into the mosaic that is America.

Every ethnic group is special, in that it has something uniquely its own to bring to the great mix that is America. But Chinese-Americans are very special, indeed, for they are one of humanity's greatest, largest, and oldest civilizations—indeed, the world's oldest continuous civilization. They are people with thousands of years of unbroken history and achievement behind them, and they have come to America with an enormous amount to offer. Their ideas, and their philosophers, historians, scientists, doctors, pharmacists, and artists have had enormous impact on all of the peoples of the world since long before the birth of Christ. The Chinese-Americans are justifiably proud of their land and its people, from whom much can be learned. Like those of so many other ethnic groups, they are also people who have much to learn and gain from the ideas of freedom, equality, and progress that are at the heart of the American dream and of the American experience.

The Immigrants

Trade between the United States and China began soon after America's Revolutionary War, when New England sailors began what would become a flood of trade and interchange between the two countries.

1

By the 1790s a trickle of Chinese immigrants to the American mainland had already begun, consisting of small numbers of students, merchants, sailors, and house servants. A somewhat larger group, mostly of merchants, settled in then-independent Hawaii, starting in the 1790s. In all, only a few hundred Chinese immigrants came to the United States and Hawaii before 1850. Almost all of them were from the South China province of Kwangtung (modern Guangdong). More precisely, most had lived in or near the great South China port city of Canton (modern Guangzhou), which in those decades was the center of Chinese trade with all foreigners coming to China by sea—as it had been since Roman times.

That trickle of Chinese immigrants into the United States grew into a wave, starting with the California Gold Rush of 1849. About 300,000 Chinese immigrants came to America between the Gold Rush and 1882, to make their fortune in the country they called the "land of the Golden Mountains." Like the earlier immigrants, almost all were from Kwangtung, coming out through the British colony of Hong Kong. Most were men. Many did find their fortunes in America, but all soon found themselves facing deep racial hatred. By the 1870s that racism had flared into murderous anti-Chinese hysteria. The result was the Chinese Exclusion Act of 1882, which was followed by many other anti-Chinese laws and "actions." These included several massacres and the driving of tens of thousands of Chinese from the land, sea, and mines into the "Chinatowns" of the American West. These Chinatowns became both prisons and refuges during the hard times that followed.

In Hawaii, things developed differently. About 50,000 Chinese immigrants came to the islands during the last half of the 19th century. The great majority of these were also from Kwangtung, though some were of the Hakka ethnic group, from farther north on the South China coast. Because Hawaii's ethnic mix and political situation were different from those of the young United States, the Hawaiian-Chinese community developed more normally than the early, mainland Chinese-American community, though not without discrimination. However, after the United States annexed Hawaii in 1898, the American exclusion laws were applied, almost completely shutting down the main Chinese immigration to Hawaii.

And so it remained, until after World War II. In those five decades a relatively small number of immigrants were able to enter America, and those with very great difficulty. Even so, the Chinese-American communities of the mainland and of Hawaii developed strongly, in spite of the discrimination and exclusion they faced, becoming unique, contributing parts of the larger American community.

In the 1950s, after the 1949 victory of the Chinese Communist forces in the Chinese Civil War, about 5,000 Chinese students and professionals were stranded in the United States. Many of them stayed, later becoming permanent residents. They were from all over China, and included many of the best educated and most highly skilled people of their time and country. They were the vanguard of the second major migration of Chinese to the United States, which started in the 1960s and continues today. This is a migration of people from all over China. Though many of them come out through Hong Kong, as they did in earlier days, now they cross the wide Pacific by airplane, rather than by boat.

The Chinese Heritage

The Chinese are one of the world's greatest peoples. Their heritage of thousands of years of unbroken civilization expresses itself in a whole

This young Chinese-American girl continues her ancestors' long and distinguished heritage as she studies the characters used in Chinese writing. (Copyright Washington Post, reprinted by permission of the D.C. Public Library)

bundle of tremendously valuable qualities and skills brought to America.

The Chinese brought the pride of a people who, since long before the birth of Christ, have considered themselves to be at the very center of the world. These are the people of the world-famous philosopher Confucius, of the renowned historian Ssu-ma Ch'ien, of the fearless explorers and conquerors of much of Asia. And they know it. The Chinese immigrants carried their pride with them to an America that tried to turn them away—once. Now they contribute that pride to a modern America that welcomes them.

They also brought courage, which is to be expected of a great people and which goes with their pride. That courage has been amply demonstrated by Chinese-Americans, who have successfully built lives, families, communities, and careers in what have often been terribly difficult conditions.

The Chinese also brought a very strong sense of family and community, which has been a deep part of the Chinese heritage for thousands of years, and continues today. This, most of all, is what carried Chinese-Americans through the hardest times in America.

Beyond that, the Chinese brought to America the willingness and ability to work hard, long, intelligently, and flexibly. In their homeland the early Chinese immigrants had mostly been farmers—some of the best of their time in the world. Many also had been skilled craftspeople, and a sprinkling were merchants. In America, they became highly skilled miners, railroad builders, botanical scientists, and much else, as well as pursuing the occupations they already knew. And in the modern world, Chinese and Chinese-Americans have resumed their places among the world's greatest scientists, medical practitioners, teachers, managers, financiers, and scholars.

Last, and far from least, they brought the ability to hope, to dream, to think long thoughts, and to plan well for the future. The Chinese have always been profound thinkers and great builders, as their Great Wall and Grand Canal so clearly show. Now Chinese-Americans build their lives and work in America, and make powerful contributions to the American future.

In the late 1980s, as we approach the last decade of the 20th century, there are well over a million Chinese-Americans in the United States. Some are descended from those early immigrants who came to San Francisco with their families in Gold Rush days. Some are the children's children's children of families reunited in the United States after being separated for many years by exclusion acts and by continuing opposition. Some are the stranded students of the 1950s, and their children, now into the third generation in America. Some of them are very new Americans, with children just beginning to grow up in America. All are Americans. All are Chinese-Americans. All mix and partially merge the long, rich heritage of old China with the much newer, equally important experience of being Americans.

2

The Center of the World

People from big, powerful countries tend to see their own lands as the center, the focus of everything in the world. Most Americans certainly feel that way about the United States; many Chinese and Soviets feel that way about their countries, too.

But for Americans and Russians, this view of their countries as being at the center of the world is a relatively new thing, dating back only a few hundred years. For the Chinese, it is a view going back at least 3,000 years. For hundreds of millions of Chinese, right up to today, China is still the center and the only truly civilized country on Earth.

Indeed, the very name of the country makes that clear. The Chinese name for their ancient land is *Chung-Kuo*. The name means "The Central Country." It can also be translated as "The Middle Kingdom," the civilized land at the center of the world, surrounded by barbarians.

In a way, this view is entirely understandable. China has been for thousands of years one of the greatest of the world's countries and cultures, as well as by far the most populous country in the world. Also, it has been a continuous, living civilization for all those thousands of years. Chinese civilization—basically the same Chinese people and culture we know today—flourished at the same time as lands we now see as only a part of ancient history. Two thousand years ago, Chinese silk was being traded for Roman and Carthaginian gold along the old Silk Road. Rome and Carthage have long since faded into the history books. But China endures.

Beginnings

China is a big country. After the Soviet Union and Canada, it is the third largest country in the world, being a little larger than the United States in land area. The Soviet Union is over twice as large as China, with 8.6 million square miles to China's almost 3.7 million square miles. Canada has almost 160,000 square miles more than China, and the United States about 76,000 square miles less.

In population, though, China is by far the largest country in the world. With over one billion people—nearly one-quarter of all humanity—it has four times as many people as either the United States or the Soviet Union, and about 40 times the population of Canada. Putting it a little differently, China has almost twice the combined population of the United States, the Soviet Union, and Canada. If you include people of Chinese background living outside China, the number is even larger, because that would include the large ethnic Chinese populations of southeast Asia, plus smaller ethnic Chinese populations all over the world.

Like so many of the world's peoples, especially the Americans, the Chinese are in fact a mosaic, a combination of many peoples. Since long before the Chinese immigration to the United States began, the dominant Chinese ethnic group as been that of the Han, who originated in North China. They and most other Chinese ethnic groups are of East Asian—often called "Mongolian"—origin, with skin coloration that mainly ranges from brown to gold, though there are also many very dark-skinned and very light-skinned Chinese. The most obvious other physical characteristic shared by most—but far from all—of the peoples of China is the *epicanthus fold*, which is a fold of the upper eyelid's skin that tends to cover the inner corner of the eye.

We do not know all the ethnic and racial groups that have contributed to the forming of the Chinese people, but we do know that they have been many and diverse in China's long history. Along with the Han, there were certainly several Mongol peoples and several Turkic-speaking peoples, as well as Manchus, Jurchens, Koreans, Tanguts, and Tibetans. There are the Miao, Mo-So, and Lo-Lo peoples. There are Khmers, Thais, Hakkas, Arabs, Jews, and a score of other peoples. China occupies a huge portion of Eurasia, the greatest land mass in the world. Its peoples have mixed and merged with the other peoples of East and Central Asia for many thousands of years.

Because Chinese governments have traditionally kept excellent records, we can be sure that today's Chinese civilization goes back in an unbroken line to at least 3,000 years ago. It probably goes back much further, but no one can be entirely sure just how far.

The evidence dug up so far—and it really is dug up, for much of it is the product of archaeological "digs," as archaeologists call them—shows that settled communities had developed in China at least 7,000 years ago. They centered on the North Chinese plain, and especially in those areas fed by the Yellow River. Chinese people were farming by then, raising farm

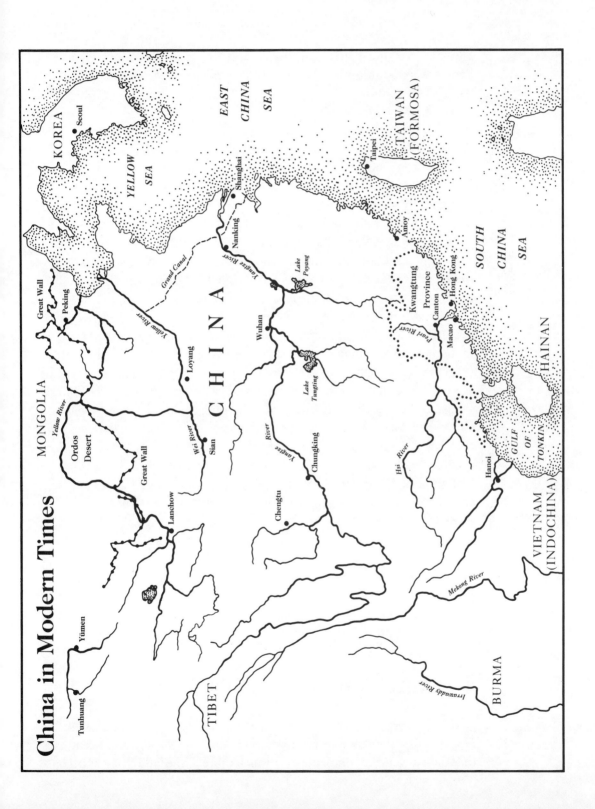

China in Modern Times

animals, creating pottery and tools, and living in communities, just as people were beginning to do far to the west, in Mesopotamia and in the countries around the Mediterranean. Recent research indicates that Chinese civilization may be 8,000 to 10,000 years old, or even older—perhaps as old as the oldest civilizations we know, in what are now Turkey, Iraq, Iran, and other countries in the Middle East.

Chinese legends tell of kingdoms—the Shang and the Yü—going back into a period 4,000 to 5,000 years ago, that is, back as far as 3000 B.C. Whether these kingdoms really existed or not, the archaeological evidence shows a considerable civilization on the North China plain at that time, complete with walled villages, or even cities, highly developed religions, and many marks of the China we know today. The North China plain continued to be the center of Chinese culture. Clearly, this region has rightly been called the cradle of Chinese civilization.

By 4,000 years ago, the Hsia dynasty had clearly emerged—the first that archaeologists can confirm, beyond legend. It lasted about 500 years, more than twice as long as the history of the United States. But there are as yet no reliable written sources from that time. Such sources begin to be available at about 2,500 years ago, with writings found on bones and shells, as well as on some pieces of jade, pottery, and bronze. Works on Chinese history often call the bone and shell writings "oracle bones" because they were used in ceremonies to communicate with royal ancestors and to foresee the future.

This was the time of the Shang dynasty, which lasted approximately another 500 years, until about 1,000 years before the birth of Christ. This was China's Bronze Age. In China, as all across Europe and Asia at that time, weapons, armor, tools, and much else were made of bronze. China's workers in bronze of that time were especially notable for the beauty of their fine storage vessels. This was also an age of the beginnings of empire. What we call "China" was still made up of many individual states. But in these centuries the rulers of Shang China gained some measure of control over much of the North China plain.

The Chou and Confucius

A neighboring state to the west, that of the Chou kings, won control of North China about 3,000 years ago. For the next two and a half centuries the Chou developed their rule over much more of the land that was becoming ancient China. They built a new capital city, Hao, near the modern city of Sian, on the Wei River. For centuries to come, China's capitals would be in this region, at Ch'ang-an (modern Sian) or a little east at Loyang. The Chou dynasty ruled their large country through a system of vassal states. The net result was a setup something like the European feudal system of 2,000 years later. The walled city was the main feature of the countryside, and peasants worked the land for lords who both exploited them and protected them against other lords and their armies. At the same time, the lords gave their allegiance and support to the Chou rulers, who ruled lightly and from a distance. Their dynasty is today known as that of the Western Chou.

In 771 B.C., they were overthrown by rebels from among their own people, in alliance with "barbarians," meaning neighboring peoples, but of basically the same racial group and Chinese history. The dynasty that resulted was called the Eastern Chou. It lasted five and a half centuries, with its capital at Loyang, on the Yellow River, about 200 miles east of modern Sian.

From very early times, China's cities were surrounded by thick, high walls and were entered only through heavily guarded gates, like this one at 19th-century Sian. (By Sven Hedin, from Through Asia, *1899)*

ONE OF THE GATES OF SI-NING-FU

This was the first great period of Chinese history and culture. Its philosophers, scientists, inventors, historians, and artists provided much of the basis for the unique and lasting heritage of China. Its extraordinarily productive and skilled peasants, workers, traders, and administrators provided a burst of energy and wealth that made ancient China truly the center of its world for over 2,000 years to come.

However, it was not a period of empire. There was a Chou dynasty, but in name only. In practice, what existed was a set of semi-independent states, many of them more powerful than the "ruling" state at Loyang. Indeed, most of the last two centuries of the Eastern Chou is known as the Warring States period. Yet at the same time it was a period of great cooperation, in which a strong, basically unified economy and people emerged in what is now North China. And a large, large people they were: By the third century B.C., 2,200 years ago, China was probably the most populous country in the world, as it has been since and is today.

In Chou times, iron was introduced into China, as it had been 600 to 700 years earlier in western Asia. That meant iron weapons, but far more importantly it meant the iron-tipped plow, which made China's industrious farmers far more productive that before. Their productivity was also greatly increased by the large-scale irrigation and canal-building projects developed throughout North China in this period. With this tremendous increase in the production of wealth, and with freedom to trade throughout the country, China had everything necessary to become a wealthy, unified land. The towns developed greatly, as did the internal silk trade. Copper coins came to be used as cash money, and silk itself became a medium of exchange, that is, a kind of money. A host of other uniquely Chinese articles were introduced, including chopsticks. Communications and commerce, knitting together the country, were also greatly helped by the widespread introduction into China and the rest of East Asia of the riding horse, and by the building of a network of transportation canals that crisscrossed the country.

But there was something else, as well, far beyond all these practical developments. For this was the greatest age of classic Chinese thought, the age that saw the development of much of the body of thinking we recognize as uniquely Chinese. To begin to understand the great Chinese heritage, we must see clearly three main things. First, the Chinese civilization is the oldest continuous civilization on the face of the earth. Second, it is a huge civilization and massive population, which has seen itself as the center of the world for thousands of years. Third, it has developed a body of think-

For thousands of years the Chinese were famous for their silk, which was grown, spun, and woven by the women of every household, including the empress herself. (Authors' archives)

ing that has deeply influenced the history of the Chinese people, and that continues to influence them in vitally important ways even today, when so much has changed in China and in the rest of the world. The tremendous Chinese willingness to work, the enormous Chinese attachment to the immediate family and the extended family, and the great respect and desire for learning—all these are central to the Chinese. They have been so for thousands of years, and such central attitudes are not made or unmade in a generation or two. These attitudes are carried by Chinese all over the world, including in the United States. To the Chinese they are as natural as breathing.

Of all the philosophers of Chou times, the most important was Confucius, whose name is really Master K'ung, or in Chinese K'ung-fu-tzu. His thinking influenced the whole history of Chinese civilization. Confucius is thought to have lived from 551 to 479 B.C. He had many schools of followers, in his lifetime and for 2.500 years beyond—to this day.

One main aspect of what Confucius taught is quite different from the main inclination of most Americans today. For he preached that the ancient ways were best, that people should bow to their ancient rulers, and that change was not to be welcomed. However, he also taught that those who ruled had a duty to practice high moral standards—which is not so far at all from the way most Americans view the obligations of people who hold high office. He also taught a whole series of desired qualities in people, including honesty, loyalty, love for humanity, and the rightness of treating others as you would like them to treat you. Those are all qualities much respected in both China and the United States, then and now. In addition he taught that it was right to be a highly cultured, "polished" person. Very important in his teaching was the idea of moderation, of balance in all things, especially between your personal core of honesty and the need to live and work with others.

Hundreds of years later, many Chinese would turn to the religion of Taoism, which focused on individual spiritual life and needs. Later still, many Chinese turned to the Buddhist religion, and quite away from the humanity-focused beliefs of Confucius. But in the end both religions lost much of their early strength, though they still remained important in China. It was the teachings of Confucius and his followers that had the deepest and longest-lasting impact on the formation of Chinese civilization and on the way individual Chinese people saw the world and their place in it.

The time of Confucius, by the way, was indeed a classic age in history. For this was also the time of the great Greek philosophers, including first Plato and later Socrates; of some of the ancient Jewish prophets; of Buddha, who in this period began to teach in India; and of Zoroaster, who founded a great religion in Persia, now Iran.

The Han Empire

After Confucius and the period of the Eastern Chou dynasty came a brief period of near-anarchy. This was quickly followed by the emergence of the first great, unified Chinese empire. Between 221 B.C. and 206 B.C., China—that is, the many states of what is now northern China—was united for the first time by the conquering Ch'in dynasty. The rule of the Ch'in was brief, but it was followed by over 400 years of the great Han dynasty.

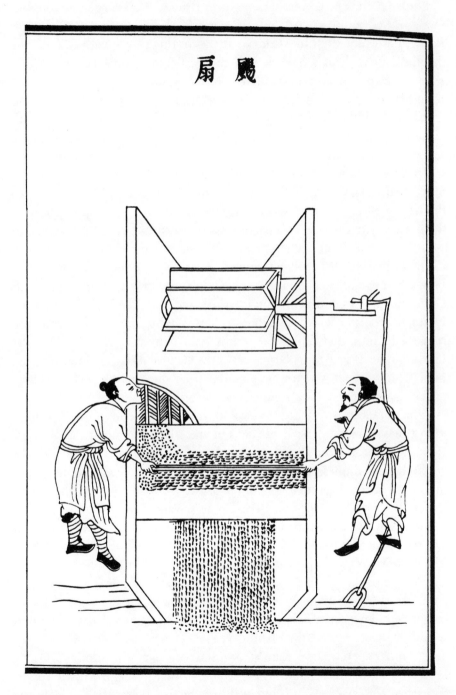

扇颺

Long skilled farmers, the Chinese have been using devices like this treadle machine for winnowing grain since at least the Han period (roughly the time of the Roman Empire). (From Thien Kung Khai Wu, 1637)

Under the Han, China became one of the world's largest, strongest, most unified empires. At the other end of the then-known world was Rome, the Rome of Julius Caesar. It was in this first great imperial age that the Chinese began to think of themselves as the "Men of Han," and of Han China as the empire at the center of the world.

In Han times, China did, indeed, become a huge country. Conquering armies spread Han rule far beyond the plains of North China. To the south and east, they conquered the land all the way to what is now Canton on the southern coast, and much of the country that is now the southern and southeastern portion of modern China. To the west, they conquered much of Central Asia, building forts and invading across Asia halfway toward the Mediterranean. Everywhere they went and ruled, they brought with them a unified Chinese culture and government.

In Han times, huge new portions of Asia became Chinese. And once Chinese, they tended to stay Chinese. Even in later centuries, when the Han Chinese empire had faded away and new rulers came, most of South China remained Chinese in ethnic origin and culture. And although the Han Chinese later withdrew from Central Asia, much Chinese influence remained, until later Chinese empires retook much of the land that the Han Chinese had ruled. A large part of the Central Asian land ruled by the Han Chinese 2,000 years ago, at the time of Christ's birth, is now Sinkiang, modern China's huge western province.

Imperial China influenced trade and travel far beyond its own borders. Han times were the first great days of the silk trade along the old Silk Road, which ran from the Han capitals of Ch'ang-an and Loyang all the way to Rome. Chinese silk for Roman gold—that was the greatest trade in the world in those centuries. And it was the Chinese who had the silk to trade; all the Romans had that the Chinese wanted or needed was gold.

Han times were also times of enormous construction in China. Han laborers built the first Great Wall along China's Mongolian borderlands. The Wall was meant to protect China from the nomadic peoples to its north and west. For thousands of years, the main invasion route into China was from out of Asia. Successive waves of invaders were either thrown back or conquered and later absorbed by the Chinese. In Han times, the main would-be invaders were the Hsiung-Nu, also known as the Eastern Huns. They and the Chinese fought a hundred-year war along China's northwestern border. The Chinese won that war, in the process adopting their enemies' cavalry tactics and building the first Great Wall. The Huns ultimately retreated across Asia, as Han Chinese power expanded to the west.

In those days of empire, China became a fully unified nation, with one main government, one main army, and one main culture. In the consciousness of most Chinese, this is what China has been for 2,000 years since—a great empire at the center of the world. Looking at it this way, it becomes easy to understand why many of the Chinese who came to the United States as immigrants felt that they were coming from a great civilization to a barbarian country. They felt that way even though 19th-century China had fallen upon hard times and was very weak. They felt that way even though many of the earliest Chinese immigrants to the United States were poor people from country places. None of it mattered: They were Chinese, the conquerors of East Asia, the children of Confucius, men of Han.

For the Chinese, Han times were a first imperial golden age—followed after 220 A.D. by hundreds of years of division, small wars between the Chinese states, and invasions from out beyond the Great Wall. There was a great deal of migration from the troubled north to the south. In those centuries, South China became a center of a massive Chinese population. It was from South China, from the area around the major port of Canton, that most of the early American Chinese emigration would come in the 19th century.

One of the most extraordinary architectural achievements of world history was the building of the 1,500-mile-long Great Wall, which guarded China's northern and western borders.
(Adapted from Peking and the Pekingese *by Dr. Rennie, from Henry Yule's* Marco Polo*)*

The Middle Ages

In the seventh century A.D., starting in 618 A.D., a new, unified China emerged—a new imperial era and a new golden age under the T'ang dynasty. During the three centuries of T'ang rule, Central Asia was reconquered, a new central government and administration ruled the country from Ch'ang-an, and another great period in Chinese art and literature flourished. This new Chinese empire stretched all the way from deep in Central Asia to the Pacific shore and from what is now Manchuria all the way south to include much of what is now Vietnam. In T'ang times, the Chinese also built the greatest canal system ever known, including the huge Grand Canal that linked rich South China with the northern borders of the empire. And once again the Chinese traded silk and other goods far to the west, by land across Asia to far-away Europe and by sea all the way around Asia and beyond to East Africa and the Mediterranean. The T'ang capital at Ch'ang-an became a worldwide cultural and trading center, with Arabs, Jews, Armenians, Persians, and many other trading and traveling peoples of the known world sending gifts and representatives to the T'ang emperor's court.

By about 900 A.D., the T'ang golden age was over. China once again broke up into a body of competing states and short-lived dynasties. But China itself did not break up; the Chinese people and their very rich economy continued to develop, although governments and northern invaders persistently came and went for the next 60 years. In 960 A.D., the Sung dynasty began, lasting three centuries, until the Mongols conquered North and then South China, starting in 1271 A.D. These were the Mongols led by Kublai Khan, grandson of the great Mongol conqueror of Asia, Genghis Khan.

With the Mongols came a new day in Asia. For the first time, most of Asia was united in a single empire. For the first time, you could travel all the way from Europe to China carrying a single pass from the Mongol government. That is exactly what Marco Polo did, traveling by land from the Mediterranean to the court of Kublai Khan and back by sea around Asia to Italy in the years 1271 through 1295 A.D. He and other travelers brought back stories that hardly anyone at first believed, about a great empire to the east. But they opened up Europe to the idea of China and started a process of trade and mutual discovery that continues into our own times.

Marco Polo called the Mongols' Chinese capital city Cambulac. That was his way of saying Khanbaligh, in Turkish meaning "The City of the Khan." Later, this great city was to be called Peking, and then Beijing. Today it is the capital of the Chinese People's Republic.

From their capital, the Mongols ruled China. First they took North China, the traditional heartland of the Han people. Soon they conquered South China as well, and made it part of their enormous empire. They nearly took Japan, too. Their first invasion of Japan failed, as all Japan united to fight the invaders at a great wall put up by the Japanese to bar the Mongol invaders. Their second, greater invasion force—much like the huge Grand Armada the Spanish put together to invade England hundreds of years later—might have succeeded, for it faced no such opposition as the English fleet. But a huge storm destroyed the Mongol armada, and changed the course of Asian and world history.

China still endured. The Mongols ruled for a hundred years, and then were forced to pull back into Central Asia. They left behind a united China, to be taken over by the Ming dynasty, in which the rulers were Chinese. Then, 300 years later, the Ming gave way to the Ch'ing dynasty, in which the rulers were the Manchus, another set of invaders from the northwest.

Through it all, though—Mongol, Ming, and Ch'ing, a period lasting in all over 600 years—China remained fully united. For all that time, the Chinese continued to be a single people, with basically a single view of themselves as a great people at the center of the world. The Chinese people have never really changed that view of China and of themselves. Not even through the extremely hard and difficult times that started in the early part of the last century and have extended right up into modern times.

Troubled Times

Late in the 18th century, many Europeans and Americans began coming to China. They made a tremendous impact during the first half of the 19th century and caused a great deal of harm. Even before that, the Russian empire had started eastward on the path of conquest that would take it right to the Pacific, and beyond to Alaska.

At the same time, the Manchus were beginning to run into internal problems. One of them was the enormous population growth in South

China during the centuries of stability. Another was the growth of considerable corruption among Chinese officials late in Manchu times, when the Europeans and Americans were beginning to make their major move into China.

That major move started as trade. Beginning in 1564, Spaniards traded west from Central and South America across the Pacific to the Philippines; there they met Chinese traders who took Spanish goods back to the mainland. Portugal established a beachhead at Macao, in 1557, on the South China mainland and secured a trade monopoly. Late in the 17th century, the British and other Europeans traded by sea to Canton, as that was the only place the Manchus opened to such trade. The British generally traded around the Southeast Asia coast from India, and the Americans came from across the Pacific. These outsiders wanted much from China but had little the Chinese really wanted. In the search for products to trade to China, the British in the late 1700s began shipping large quantities of opium from India into China. This had disastrous effects on millions of Chinese, who quickly became addicted to the powerful drug. When the Chinese government tried to stop the opium trade, the British went to war against China. This was the Opium War of 1839-1842.

The British won the Opium War very easily, for in the centuries since Marco Polo Europe had gone far ahead of China in its military ability. China had been for all those centuries a huge, stable country, with by far the largest population in the world. It had also been a country in which many important things were invented, including printing, gunpowder, and the compass. It was a country of great scientific and historical accomplishments. But it was also a country that had not developed the ability to make modern war. Its navy was almost useless against modern British warships. Its forts could not stand up against modern naval guns. Its disorganized, old-fashioned Manchu army did well against poorly armed Central Asian nomad peoples, but could not fight effectively against well armed European soldiers and sailors.

The result of all this was that the British were able to completely defeat the Chinese forces and occupy cities and forts from Hong Kong and Canton all the way north to Shanghai. Finally, the Chinese asked for peace and signed a treaty that "opened" six ports to European commerce. Further unequal treaties followed, with the British, French, Americans, Russians, and others. China was to be victimized by these foreign powers for most of the following century. They held special, unequal trading rights, and forced China to pay huge money penalties again and again. They also occupied their own sections in some of China's major cities, such as the International Settlement in Shanghai. Most foreign citizens were not even subject to Chinese laws.

The adverse impact of all this on the proud Chinese—and on the already weak Manchu government—was enormous. Anti-foreign feeling grew tremendously in China. Anti-Manchu feeling also grew, as new ideas began to move through the country. China, so stable for over six centuries, began to come apart. The late 1840s saw the beginning of a long series of rebellions and full-scale civil wars. These only ended a full century later with the victory of the Communist Chinese forces and the establishment of the present Chinese government.

The earliest, large popular rebellions against the Manchus came in the late 1840s, in and around Canton. This is not at all surprising, for the Canton region had long been the main entry port for foreigners coming into China. During all the centuries since the Manchus had ended the last of the Chinese dynasties, the Ming, Canton had also been a longtime center of anti-Manchu feeling. The Triad Society, which had begun as an anti-Manchu fighting organization, was very strong in this part of South China. It and many of the other secret societies that existed in the China of the time were also heavily involved in many kinds of illegal activities. These secret societies were to survive for a very long time, even until today. As time went by, they were to become less patriotic and more criminal, much like the Sicilian Mafia. In their own way and place, they were just as strong as the Mafia. The region around Canton was also the home of Sun Yat-Sen, the great leader of the successful final revolution against the Manchus that established the Republic of China. It was from this part of South China, with its long exposure to Westerners and its century-long turmoil starting in the late 1840s, that most of the early Chinese immigration to America came. To understand who they were that came to America and why they came, it is vital to know first that these early immigrants were far from being the dull, ignorant peasants that some anti-Chinese bigots later made them out to be.

In the early 1850s, a great rebellion occurred, which soon led to a major civil war. This was the Taiping Rebellion, in which over 20 million Chinese lives were lost in a war that lasted almost 15 years. During the course of that massive civil war, the British and French took first one side and then the other, always pursuing their own aims. In the late 1850s, they successfully made war against the Manchus, taking Peking in 1860 and forcing further unequal treaties on the Chinese government. Then in the early 1860s, the Europeans helped the Manchus defeat the Taiping armies, and further built their position in China.

It was during this long time of great troubles that the earliest major Chinese immigration came to America, part of a much larger emigration out of China to many countries. And now we turn to the coming of the Chinese to America.

3

Out of China

The art and science of writing history is highly developed in China. As early as 2,100 years ago, one of the greatest of the world's historians, Ssu-ma Ch'ien, wrote a massive history of China up until that time. After him, the study and writing of history became one of the most respected of Chinese occupations.

Because the Chinese value historical writings so highly, we must pay very careful attention to early Chinese writings about a land far to the east, visited by Chinese Buddhist priests late in the fifth century A.D. *The Great Chinese Encyclopedia*, written early in the sixth century, describes their journey. As the story goes, the party, which was led by the priest Hui Shen, landed somewhere on the West Coast of what is now North America, and then traveled along the coast south to what is now Mexico. They called the country they found *Fusang*.

It is possible that such a journey really happened, as the Chinese were a great seafaring people, and their ships could have made the trip across the Pacific. If so, they would have arrived in North America several centuries before the Vikings, and a thousand years before Columbus. On the other hand, until now there has been little other evidence of any such Chinese voyage, and no discovery of any lasting Chinese settlements in what would later become the United States, Canada, and Mexico.

There has been a good deal of research and speculation about the trip to Fusang, and about possible other, later Chinese voyages to North America, but no real proof of such a journey.

The China Trade

In more modern times, the first Chinese probably came to the Americas with Spanish traders. Even though little hard evidence exists, at least some

During the years of the China trade, Chinese artists often learned to paint pictures that would appeal to European or American audiences, like that of the junk—an Asian sailing ship—above right. (From The World: Its Cities and Peoples, *19th century)*

Chinese probably traveled east on the Spanish galleons going back to Mexico from the Philippines, during the early days of Spain's China trade. Many of the Spanish ships were built in the Philippines, by crews that included skilled Chinese shipbuilders. Also, most of those trading with the Spanish in the Philippines were Chinese, who then took their Spanish silver and goods back to China. It is very reasonable to guess that some adventurous Chinese sailors found their way to Mexico in those early years. It is even possible to believe, as some have claimed, that there were Chinese with adopted Spanish names among the early Spanish explorers of California. There were certainly some Chinese in Spanish California by the middle of the 18th century, working as shipbuilders and domestic workers.

After the American Revolution, the new American nation began what was to become the great China Trade. These were the days of sailing ships and long journeys, before the building of the Panama Canal. In those days, New England ships made a long, long journey all the way around South America past Cape Horn, and then 7,000 miles more across the Pacific to China. Often, the journey was even longer than that, for the American ships usually made stops in the Pacific to pick up such trade goods as Alaskan furs to exchange with the Chinese.

These American ships brought back such goods as silk and superbly made Chinese ceramics and carved wooden furniture. They also began to bring back Chinese—just a few, but the first Chinese to come to the new United States. As early as 1785, Chinese crewmen were reported to be on ships returning from the Far East. Before 1800, a few more Chinese had entered the United States. Five arrived in Philadelphia as house servants with a Dutch family in 1796.

Chinese also continued to arrive in California, which was then a Spanish colony. It would not become a part of the United States until 1850, after the Gold Rush of 1849 brought large numbers of Americans to California.

By far the largest group of Chinese to arrive in California in the early years came with the Meares expedition. In 1788, British captain John Meares sailed from the area around Canton to Vancouver Island, heading a party that included many Chinese sailors as well as several kinds of skilled builders. There, on Vancouver Island, they built a fort that was also a trading post, and a sailing ship named the *Northwest America*, for trading along the coast. The next year, in 1789, about 75 more Chinese arrived, brought by Captains Meares and Metcalf. Some historians doubt that all of the people who came from East Asia to this settlement were Chinese, but there is little doubt that this was the first substantial group of Chinese to settle on the West Coast. Unfortunately, the Spanish claimed that whole coast, and saw the settlement as a threat. They sailed north in force and closed the settlement. No one is clear as to how many of these early Chinese settlers found their way back to China, stayed in California, or went south to Mexico.

During the next 60 years, only a few more Chinese entered either the United States or Spanish California. Five Chinese students, the first of what would in later years become many thousands, arrived to study at a religious mission school in Cornwall, Connecticut, between 1818 and 1825. Three more Chinese students arrived in 1847. One of them was Yung Wing, who graduated from Yale in 1854. He later became an important person in China, and was greatly responsible for sending large numbers of Chinese students to study in America.

In 1847, a whole Chinese crew sailed the *Keying*, a Chinese junk—a kind of sailing ship—from China to New York. There is no record that any of the Chinese crew stayed in América, but the visit attracted a great deal of American attention.

A few other Chinese came to America before the late 1840s, but only a few. Up until 1820, no reliable United States immigration records were kept, and the information available on Chinese immigration into Spanish California is also sketchy, at best. The United States records show a total of 45 Chinese arrivals—that is, of those who had arrived and been counted at Atlantic and Gulf Coast ports—in the United States between 1820 and 1850. That is probably an undercounting, but the numbers were surely very small.

These early Chinese who came to America were visitors and students, rather than immigrants who came to work in America. There was substantial emigration out of China during the first part of the 19th century, but the emigrants were mostly bound for other places in south Asia and around the Indian Ocean, rather than across the Pacific.

The Manchu Chinese government had long forbidden emigration, with severe criminal penalties—including death—for those who were caught trying to leave. But as the Manchu dynasty weakened, so did its ability to prevent emigration. At the same time, its very weakening created more reasons to leave the country in search of a living.

A Time of Troubles

Until the middle of the 19th century, few Chinese saw any very good reason for coming to America. China was 7,000 miles from the West Coast, and that coast was very lightly settled by the Spanish. There were no great opportunities for making a living in Spanish California. That is why even the stories of those who returned from the United States failed to set off any kind of mass move to go to America. By contrast, immigrants from northern Europe in the same years had many good reasons to come to America; they were coming to the flourishing East Coast of the young United States looking for jobs, land, and freedom. And what they found caused them to write back home and also send money for others to come. That is how "American fever" developed in country after country in Europe. Before large numbers of Chinese would want to come to America, something would have to happen.

Something did. Two things, actually: one back home in China and one far across the Pacific, in America.

What happened in China was a sudden, sharp worsening of the situation in the southern part of the country. First there was the opium trade, which created millions of opium addicts in China, and greatly weakened the whole economy. Then there was the Opium War that the British started to maintain and expand the opium trade. When that war was lost by China, an already weak Chinese government was made even weaker and official corruption increased. China had also seen tremendous population increases, which made it ever more difficult to make a living. Then, in the 1840s, popular rebellions broke out, some of which were centered in Kwangtung province, where almost all of the Chinese immigrants to America came from. And, starting in 1850, there was the enormous Chinese civil war called the Taiping Rebellion, in which over 20 million people died and scores of millions more were wounded or made homeless. In all those circumstances, it became very difficult, indeed, for most people to make a living in South China.

It is not surprising that in those times millions of Chinese immigrated to other countries. In the early years, most went to Southeast Asia, some went to South America and the Caribbean, and a few tens of thousands to the United States. The flow of emigrants out of China continued through the century. The total coming to the United States finally reached about 300,000, though many of these eventually went back home to China.

Many others traveled back and forth from America to their homes in China, as did so many workers of other nationalities.

Mountains of Gold

What happened in the United States, just as China's time of troubles came, was the California gold strike. In January 1848, at John Augustus Sutter's new mill on the American River, near Sacramento, California, millwright James Marshall picked up a gold nugget out of the water. There turned out to be enormous amounts of gold in the area, enough to fuel the biggest gold rush in history. By the following year, 1849, hundreds of thousands of goldseekers had arrived from all over the world. They were to be called the Forty-niners, after the year the first huge wave arrived in California.

Many came by land, across the eastern United States to the Missouri River, and then 2,000 miles more on the old Oregon-California trail, opening the American West as they came. Others came across the Southwest. A great many came by sea from the East, some coming all the way around South America and most going by ship to Panama, by land across Panama, and then by ship again, up the coast to California.

And some came from China, 7,000 miles away across the Pacific. Emigration out of China was then in full swing. Word filtered back to China of the land the Chinese came to call Gum San—the Mountains of Gold. Soon some of the hardiest and most adventurous people in the country made up their minds to come to America.

Most of the early emigrants from Kwangtung came from the small, six-county area around the Pearl River Delta. Canton is the big central city of the region and the foreign-held cities of Hong Kong and Macao are nearby.

These emigrants were people who had had much contact with Americans and Europeans. They were, in that way, quite different from most other Chinese. As much as anything else, it was that previous contact that made the immigration to America possible. For all of China, the middle of the 19th century was a time of great troubles, but few Chinese from other areas even tried to reach America and its "mountains of gold." It was not a matter of the people of Kwangtung being a sailing people while other Chinese were not. Far from it. There were sailors all up and down the long China coast. Many of them had, by then, been trading out of Shanghai, with the Spanish in the Philippines, for hundreds of years.

It is not completely clear, even now, exactly why the Chinese immigrants to America came from such a limited area, even though we know that there were hard times and civil war all over China and mass emigration out of China to many places. But at least we do know that news of the American gold strike came back to the people of Kwangtung from the relatively small number of Chinese in California at the time. And we do know that these were the people who knew the Westerners best, and often worked with them, in Canton, Hong Kong and Macao.

Many of the early Chinese immigrants to America came from the lands near Canton and had lived in farmhouses like these along the Pearl River Delta. (From The Far East and the New America, *by G. Waldo Browne, 1901)*

The Immigrant Chain

We also know, from the history of many other immigrant groups, that there is a pattern to such migrations. In group after group—British, Irish, Germans, Scandinavians, Jews, Italians, Poles, and a score of other peoples—the pattern was the same. First, a few people came to America. They wrote home about their experiences, often also sending money for others to come and to support families left behind. Then more came, and eventually many more, as the word began to spread, and "immigrant chains" linking together many groups of immigrants began to form. Soon, what has often been called an "American fever" swept whole areas and even whole countries.

This "immigrant chain" pattern was especially strong among the Chinese who came to America. That is because Chinese people in those times lived in very tightly knit family groups, clans, and district associations. Most worked in trade guilds, composed of people all working in the same trade. Most also had close ties to their homeland, shared religious beliefs, and had every intention of coming back to their families, to live out their lives and die in China. All that added up to continuing strong links between those who came to America and those who stayed behind. Families, groups, associations, and guilds on both sides of the Pacific continued on, even though individuals moved 7,000 miles away to a new country. Those who left China for America did not leave all those groups behind. Quite the opposite. Right off the boat in San Francisco, Chinese immigrants were greeted by representatives of these groups in the American-Chinese community.

In one Chinese county, Toishan (also Hoishan), this immigrant chain was so strong that it brought a large portion of the male population to America during the 33 years between the beginning of the Gold Rush and the restriction of Chinese immigration. In those years, a huge number of Chinese immigrants came from that single, hilly county in the Pearl River delta. It is hard to tell just how many came and stayed, because so many traveled back and forth between the two countries, but at least 50,000 people from Toishan took passage to America in those years.

For all that, not very many Chinese came to America. Some bigoted people of that time—and some since—have spoken of "yellow hordes" of Chinese immigrants to America. But that was always untrue. The truth is that out of the whole population of China—in the 1850s over 400 million people—several million emigrated all over the world. But only a few hundred thousand Chinese came to America, and that was far less than the number that came from many European countries in the same period. During the 19th century, for example, well over four million Germans and well over three million Irish immigrated to the United States.

There is another untruth that usually comes side by side with the "yellow hordes" story. This is the charge that the Chinese who came to America were ignorant, unclean "coolies," who worked for next to nothing and forced American workers out of their jobs with unfair competition. As we discuss Chinese workers in America in later chapters, we will confront the charges about taking American jobs. Here, we will look only at the "coolie" question.

The word "coolie" itself means those who do "bitter work." It was applied to some large groups of Chinese laborers who were shipped to Cuba, South America, and some other places in the Americas and Southeast Asia as contract laborers. These laborers—really little more than slaves—were drawn from far more depressed areas than Kwantung. Many came from Fukien (modern Fujian), to the north of Kwangtung. Others were homeless people, sometimes deeply in debt, drawn from many places along the coast and inland. Many more were people who were fooled by dishonest labor agents into thinking they were emigrating as free laborers. A very large proportion had actually been kidnapped into this slavery. Indeed, many of the contract laborers who found themselves on crowded, unsanitary "coolie" ships bound across the Pacific protested bitterly. Some mutinied, rather than accept their lot. Those trapped into work as coolies on plantations were, indeed, headed for bitter work and tragic lives. Many died on the way, for conditions on the coolie ships were terrible. On arrival, those who survived found themselves working for next to nothing in hot, unhealthy plantation jobs, with poor food and inhuman working conditions. Tens of thousands died; others worked for years, and often lifetimes, as slaves. A few eventually were able to buy their way out.

Twenty-six years after he had come to America as a young student, Yung Wing was employed by the Chinese Government to "proceed to Peru at once, to look into the conditions of the Chinese coolies there." He did so, and accompanied his report with photographs secretly taken on the scene:

My report was accompanied with two dozen photographs of Chinese coolies, showing how their backs had been lacerated and torn, scarred and disfigured by the lash. I had these photographs taken in the night, unknown to anyone except the victims themselves, who were, at my request, collected and assembled together for the purpose. I knew that these photographs would tell a tale of cruelty and inhumanity perpetrated by the owners of haciendas, which would be beyond cavil and dispute.

The Peruvian Commissioner, who was sent out to China to negotiate a treaty with Viceroy Li Hung Chang to continue the coolie traffic to Peru, was still in Tientsin waiting for the arrival of my report. A friend of mine wrote me that he had the hardihood to deny the statements in my report, and said that they could not be supported by facts. I had written to the Viceroy beforehand that he should hold the photographs in reserve, and keep them in the background till the Peruvian had exhausted all his arguments, and then produce them. My correspondent wrote me that the Viceroy followed my suggestion, and the photographs proved to be so incontrovertible and palpable that the Peruvian was taken by surprise and dumbfounded. He retired completely crestfallen.

Since our reports on the actual conditions of Chinese coolies in Cuba and Peru were made, no more coolies have been allowed to leave China for those countries. The traffic had received its death blow.

But those coolies were not the Chinese who came to America. Nor did those who came to America work under such contracts or in such conditions. The Chinese who came to America from that small section of Kwangtung were free people. They were small farmers and skilled workers, such as are to be found in the small towns and villages of many countries, including the United States. Many were people who had left the land and gone to work for merchants in and around Canton and Hong Kong. They were mostly young, adventurous, and willing to borrow the money they needed for the passage to America, in hope of finding far better-paying work than was then available in China.

The emigrants out of China to America were almost entirely men in those early years, and that would be so for decades, all through the first main wave of Chinese-American immigration. Most of them were married, and had left their families back in China. As was so for many emigrants from Europe, then and later on, most of the early Chinese immigrants came to work and to earn enough to pay for passage, support themselves, and send money back home to bring others and help support their families there. Very few women came, for women in China then were rarely wage earners and were quite restricted to their home places.

During the mid-19th century, Chinese were free to enter the United States. In 1868, American envoy Anson Burlingame negotiated a key treaty with the Manchu government of China. The Burlingame Treaty provided for free immigration both ways between the United States and China. It also guaranteed protection of the rights of American and Chinese citizens in each others' countries. It also made it impossible for Chinese and Americans to become citizens of each others' countries. That had little effect on Americans, few of whom wanted to become Chinese citizens. But it had a great effect on Chinese-American immigrants, who might have wanted to become American citizens.

But in 1880, the United States renegotiated the treaty with the now very weak Chinese government. The new treaty kept American privileges in China, but made it possible for the United States to "suspend" the immigration of Chinese "laborers" into the United States.

That opened the floodgates of bigotry. By 1882, Congress had passed the Chinese Exclusion Act. Under this act, the immigration of Chinese laborers was to be halted for 10 years. In the anti-Chinese climate of the time, immigration authorities were soon labeling many skilled workers,

Foreign influences in China are strikingly symbolized by this French cathedral towering over the rough-and-tumble wharf buildings and junks of the port of Canton. (From The Far East and the New America, *by G. Waldo Browne, 1901)*

professionals, and businesspeople coming from China as "laborers," and refusing them admission to the United States.

In 1884, a second Chinese Exclusion Act was passed by Congress. Four years after that, in 1888, the Scott Act blocked the return to America of 20,000 Chinese who had gone back to China, many of them to visit their families. Some 600 Chinese-Americans actually on their way back across the Pacific to the United States were denied entry because of the passage of this law.

Four years after that, in 1892, the Geary Act extended the ban on Chinese immigration for another 10 years. The Chinese Exclusion Act also became law in Hawaii in 1898 and in the Philippines in 1902.

These anti-Chinese laws continued in effect throughout the early part of the 20th century. In 1921 and 1924, Chinese immigration was even further restricted by passage of the major general immigration laws of the time, which remained in force until mid-century. Relatively few Chinese immigrants were able to enter the United States in these difficult years, though the pressure to emigrate continued. The lucky few generally made their way through the port of Hong Kong to seek opportunity in the Land of the Golden Mountains.

4

Across the Pacific

For centuries, the Manchus forbade emigration out of China and let very few foreigners into the country. The standard penalty for trying to illegally leave the country was beheading. That was also the standard penalty for those trying to come back after illegal emigration. Understandably then, few people left illegally while the Manchus ruled China.

But as the Manchus weakened and foreign contacts grew, these penalties came to be less and less enforced. They were still on the books, however, when the first large groups of Chinese sailed to the United States in Gold Rush days. For that reason, they did not sail from Canton, which would have been the natural exit port from China. Instead, they generally left from Hong Kong, which had become a British colony after the Opium War. Some also sailed from the Portuguese colony of Macao, across the wide bay at the mouth of the Pearl River. Canton is upstream some miles from the two colonies and the counties from which most of the emigrants came were on both sides of the river.

Some ships carrying Chinese emigrants did sail from Canton, as did others from Amoy (modern Xiamen), north on the coast of Fukien province. But these were coolie ships, carrying those unfortunates who had been kidnapped or drawn in some other way into coolie trade. In those ports, and in others up and down the China coast, corrupt local officials, labor recruiters, and coolie ship captains together created and kept up the terrible coolie trade.

Macao, too, was a coolie trade port. That was why most free Chinese emigrants far preferred to leave from Hong Kong. The British in Hong Kong very early outlawed the coolie trade and kept coolie ships out of their port. They recognized the coolie trade as really no better than the slave trade, and they had taken the lead in outlawing the slave trade earlier in the 19th century. Leaving from Macao, a free Chinese emigrant might even pay for his passage, only to find himself on a coolie ship bound for Cuba or Peru. Or he might be kidnapped right off the streets of the city and put on such a coolie ship. Early 19th-century immigrant student Yung Wing remembered how it was in Macao:

One of the first scenes I had seen on my arrival in Macao in 1855 was a string of poor Chinese coolies tied to each other by their queues and led into one of the barracoons [poor hotels] like abject slaves. Once, while in Canton, I had succeeded in having two or three kidnappers arrested, and had them put into wooden collars weighing forty pounds, which the culprits had to carry night and day for a couple of months as a punishment for their kidnapping.

The *queues* that Yung Wing mentions were the men's own hair, worn long and braided into a hip-length single pigtail. During Manchu times, Chinese men were required to wear such pigtails as symbols of allegiance to the Manchus, and cutting them off was severely punished by law. That is why Chinese men who had emigrated abroad resisted cutting off their queues: To reappear in China without a queue was an indirect admission of illegally leaving the country, and also an illegal act in itself. Without a queue, a Chinese man could not in Manchu times go home to China, but would instead have to wait, sometimes years, until the queue was regrown.

After the Chinese revolution of 1911, which swept away the Manchus and established the Republic of China, Chinese-Americans and overseas Chinese in all countries rejoiced—and cut off their queues.

Leaving from Hong Kong, an emigrant could be reasonably sure to be aboard a ship of free people headed for the Mountains of Gold, and on the way to San Francisco. Not that conditions were always good on these ships, but at least he was not headed for slavery.

A Costly Journey

For poor immigrants from China, the trip to America was a very costly one. In the middle of the 19th century, the trip from Hong Kong or Macao to San Francisco might cost about $50, sometimes a little less. At the height of the Gold Rush frenzy, however, it might cost a great deal more, even up to $200, as captains and agents took advantage of early Chinese gold-seekers anxious to travel to the Mountains of Gold.

Today, that $50 for passage to America does not sound like much. But for the poor Chinese in China it was an enormous amount. Even for Chinese working in America, it was a great deal. When your whole pay is $1 to $2 a week, as it was for many Chinese in America, it might take years to save enough to repay money borrowed for passage. And there were other expenses as well, such as the money spent while waiting in one of the Chinese port cities for a ship to America. In the early years, it was not unusual for the total cost of the trip to come to $100—a great deal of money for Chinese immigrants in those days.

Very few of the immigrants were even close to having that much money to pay for passage. And so they raised the money in a variety of ways. Some fortunate immigrants were able to raise it through their families, with everyone supplying a little money. The money would be repaid with what was earned in America, and more besides, to support those left behind and to pay for others who wanted to come to America. That was the classic pattern developed by so many families all over the world, not just in China.

Other immigrants borrowed the money from family or district associations in China, and repaid the money later out of American earnings. Money so borrowed was almost always repaid, for the immigrants had a strong sense of responsibility to their families and associations, both in China and in America. On both sides of the Pacific, these ties were at the center of Chinese life. To fail to repay was to run the risk of becoming an outcast.

Many Chinese immigrants raised passage money by making "credit ticket agreements" with American employers. The employers would send agents to China to recruit workers and would advance the money for passage as part of a labor contract. The terms of the contract would provide that the immigrant would work for that employer for a stated time, usually ranging from three to seven years. The wages to be paid were also stated, as were the hours to be worked. The employer would deduct money each month until passage was paid for.

These "contract labor" agreements were very commonly entered into by emigrants from many nations, up until the late 19th century. They were, however, opposed by American labor, which was beginning to organize itself into unions. Union members felt that these contracts, by freezing

In the mid-19th century, after the discovery of gold in California, Chinese emigrants from the region around Canton flocked to ships that would take them on a two-month trip to Gum San, *the Land of the Golden Mountains. (California Historical Society)*

wages at low rates for many years, created unfair competition by low-paid immigrant workers. Eventually, labor's opposition to "contract labor" became so strong that the United States Congress passed laws refusing entry to immigrants coming to American jobs under such contracts. Some people used labor's opposition to contract labor as an excuse for widespread bigotry directed against Chinese immigrants, although European immigrants working as contract laborers were seldom singled out for discrimination because of it.

Such contract labor was nothing like slavery, or even like the semi-slavery suffered by many indentured servants earlier in the history of the United States. The Chinese who came to America were a free people, who remained free in America. Those working as contract laborers worked on through, paid off their debts, and moved on into their lives in America, just as those who had otherwise paid for their passage.

Sailing to America

In the Gold Rush days of 1848-50 and ensuing years, large numbers of sailing ships of every kind headed across the Pacific for San Francisco. Every available ship was pressed into service, from large, well-maintained clipper ships all the way down to small, ill-kept, badly captained vessels that could barely make the journey. Some individual Chinese even tried the trip in 30-foot junks, and two of them are reported to have made it all the way to San Francisco.

Conditions aboard these ships varied widely. Even though the emigrants were paying passengers, some of the vessels were run no better than the coolie ships, with Chinese passengers jammed into narrow bunks three deep in airless cargo holds. In those conditions, many died, for the journey in those years often took two months or more, and contagious diseases had a long time to take hold.

Many other ships came through with their precious immigrant cargos unharmed. A great deal depended on the captain and the kind of crew and ship he ran. In the same period that the *Libertad* came into San Francisco as a "fever ship," Captain Robertson of the *Balmoral* arrived at the port of San Francisco with his cargo of Chinese immigrants unharmed. A pennant flew from the mast, expressing the gratitude of the Chinese for a safe and humane crossing.

In his book, *Reminiscences*, Chinese immigrant Huie Kin tells how it was on his journey to America:

Finally, the day was set for the ship to sail. We were two full months or more on our way. I do not know what route we took, but it was warm all the time, and we stopped at no intermediate port. When the wind was good and strong, we made much headway. But for days there would be no wind, the sails and ropes would hang lifeless from the masts, and the ship would drift idly on the smooth sea, while the sailors amused themselves by fishing. Occasionally, head winds became so strong as to force us back. Once we thought we were surely lost, for it was whispered around that the officers had lost their bearings. There was plenty of foodstuff on board, but fresh water was scarce and was carefully rationed. Not a drop was allowed to be wasted for washing our faces, and so, when rain came we eagerly caught the rain water and did our washing.

On a clear, crisp, September morning in 1868, or the seventh year of our Emperor T'ung Chih, the mists lifted, and we sighted land for the first time since we left the shores of Kwangtung [Guangdong] over sixty days before. To be actually at the "Golden

This view of conditions aboard the Alaska *shows the typical overcrowding of immigrant ships that led to so much disease and death on the voyage between China and California. (Bancroft Library)*

Gate" of the land of our dreams! The feeling that welled up in us was indescribable. I wonder whether the ecstasy before the Pearly Gates of the Celestial City above could surpass what we felt at the moment we realized that we had reached our destination. We rolled up our bedding, packed our baskets, straightened our clothes, and waited.

Immigrants or visiting students headed for the East Coast of North America had even more difficult journeys ahead of them, for they had to cross *two* oceans. Heading eastward from China, their sailing ships would cross the Pacific. But, in those days before the building of the Panama Canal, they then had to travel south all the way to Cape Horn at the tip of South America. After rounding—or, as sailors would say, "doubling"—the Cape, they would travel north through the Atlantic Ocean to the East Coast of North America.

The other route took immigrants south from China, then southwest across the Indian Ocean, around the Cape of Good Hope at the tip of Africa, and then northwestward across the Atlantic, with perhaps a reprovisioning stop at the island of St. Helena, to reach the United States. Chinese student Yung Wing, in a book written late in his life, recalled his journey to America in 1847, sailing around the Cape of Good Hope in a gale:

We had the northeast trade wind in our favor, which blew strong and steady all the way from Whompoa [on the China coast] to St. Helena. There was no accident of any kind, excepting a gale as we doubled the Cape of Good Hope. The tops of the masts and ends of the yards were tipped with balls of electricity. The strong wind was howling and whistling behind us like a host of invisible Furies. The night was pitch dark and the electric balls dancing on the tips of the yards and tops of the masts, back and forth and from side to side like so many infernal lanterns in the black night, presented a spectacle never to be forgotten by me . . .

After the Cape was doubled, our vessel ploughed through the comparatively smooth waters of the Atlantic until we reached the island of St. Helena where we were obliged to stop for fresh water and provisions. . . . St. Helena, as viewed from shipboard, presented an outward appearance of a barren volcanic rock as though freshly emerged from the baptism of fire and brimstone. Not a blade of grass could be seen on its burnt and charred surface. . . . We found among the sparse inhabitants a few Chinese who were brought there by the East India Company's ships. . . .

From St. Helena we took a northwesterly course and struck the Gulf Stream, which, with the wind still fair and favorable, carried us to New York in a short time. We landed in New York on the 12th of April, 1847, after a passage of 98 days of unprecedented fair weather.

The Age of Steam

As steamships began to replace sailing ships on the oceans of the world, the trip to America became easier and less expensive. The steamships were faster, more reliable, and soon much, much larger than the sailing ships they had replaced. In 1850, some 44 ships left Hong Kong bound for America. In all, they carried about 500 Chinese immigrants. Twenty years later, a single steamship might carry twice that number, and some steamships carried well over 1,000 Chinese immigrants.

The Pacific Mail Steamship Company started carrying Chinese immigrants in 1866. Soon there were competitors. The result was to drive ticket prices far down and make it much easier for Chinese to immigrate to America. With steamships, the voyage to America might in some periods cost as little as $13. The voyage home to China might cost as little as $10.

In a steamship, the voyage might take as little as a month, and include a stop for coal and supplies at Hawaii, then known as the Sandwich Islands. The Chinese knew Hawaii as the Sandalwood Mountains, because there had been a lively export of Hawaiian sandalwood to China from about 1790 to about 1830, when the Hawaiian sandalwood forests had been used up by the traders.

Conditions aboard the immigrant steamships were often little better than they had been on the immigrant sailing ships. There was still terrible overcrowding, since the steamship companies tried to make as much money as they could out of the immigrant trade, and without any real regard for the welfare of the immigrants. The companies' attitude was not limited to the Chinese, for poor immigrants of all nations were packed into "steerage" as tightly as possible and shipping companies in both the Atlantic and the Pacific fed them as cheaply as possible.

In the immigrant neighborhoods, new arrivals would find others from their homeland, who spoke their language and would guide them into their new lives. (From Frank Leslie's Sunday Magazine, *March 1881; Library of Congress)*

"Steerage" was the upper cargo hold of the ship. Usually it was terribly crowded, had little air, and pitched and rolled a good deal on the long ocean voyage. But in a big steamship, and even with overcrowding, the voyage was often better and almost always took far less time than it had in a little sailing ship.

Arriving in America

For the new Chinese immigrants, America was a very strange place indeed. Except for the few who had actually worked directly with Westerners in and around Canton, the whole experience was new. There were different customs, buildings, foods, and ways of dressing, a very different language, and much more. Most Chinese also faced the difficult adjustment of moving from the country to the city. (That was so for many European immigrants, as well.)

The normal immigrant response was to band together in ethnic neighborhoods, like New York's huge, early Jewish community on the Lower East Side, New York's Little Italy, Chicago's Polish community, and San Francisco's Chinatown. Many of the old neighborhoods survive still, though much smaller than they were in their early days. The Chinese communities survived more fully than most. This, as we shall see, was largely because the Chinese were soon to be pushed into them as a result of discrimination.

For the Chinese, the early ethnic community was very strong. Chinese immigrants arriving in San Francisco were greeted by representatives of their own district associations and were immediately taken into the Chinese community. Here is how Huie Kin remembers it:

> In those days there were no immigration laws or tedious examinations; people came and went freely. Somebody had brought to the pier large wagons for us. Out of the general babble, someone called out in our local dialect, and, like sheep recognizing the voice only, we blindly followed, and soon were piling into one of the waiting wagons. Everything was so strange and so exciting that my memory of the landing is just a big blur. The wagon made its way heavily over the cobblestones, turned some corners, ascended a steep climb, and stopped at a kind of clubhouse, where we spent the night.

Later, I learned that people from the various districts had their own benevolent societies, with headquarters in San Francisco's Chinatown. As there were six of them, they were known as the "Six Companies." Newcomers were taken care of until relatives came to claim them and pay the bill. The next day our relatives from Oakland took us across the bay to the little Chinese settlement there, and kept us until we found work.

In later years, arrival in America was not quite so smooth and simple. During the 28 years after passage of the Chinese Exclusion Act of 1882, Chinese immigrants arriving in San Francisco were detained for indefinite periods, supposedly for immigration hearings, in a ramshackle pierside building called The Shed. This was nothing more than a two-story, broken-down warehouse on the Pacific Mail Steamship wharf. Men were held on one floor of the building, women on the other. Food and sanitary conditions were terrible, as was the overcrowding. In some periods, immigrants were detained for months, in conditions at least as appalling as those on the worst immigrant ships. The Shed was so bad that many suicides occurred there in the 28 years of its operation, so bad that its existence was one of the prime causes of China's boycott of American-made goods in 1905.

Angel Island

The detention quarters were changed in 1910—but not much for the better. This was the era of the infamous Angel Island.

Angel Island is a place. It is also a bad memory that stands for the worst of times for Chinese-Americans.

Angel Island is a small island in San Francisco Bay. From 1910 to 1940, it was used as an immigration station by the United States Immigration and Naturalization Service. It is often compared with Ellis Island, the great Golden Door, through which poured tens of millions of immigrants mostly from Europe, in the great days of American immigration.

But the comparison is unsound. Ellis Island was a gateway to America. Some were turned back at Ellis Island, but the overwhelming majority of

As anti-Chinese feeling grew, immigrants underwent increasingly long and difficult inspection procedures on arrival in America, as here at San Francisco's Custom House. (From Harper's Weekly, February 3, 1877; Library of Congress)

In the early 1900s, Chinese immigrants to San Francisco were held on arrival, for days, weeks, months, or even years, at the hostile, cheerless inspection station at Angel Island. (California Historical Society)

those who arrived there came right on through. At Angel Island, the main intention was to keep Chinese immigrants out. That is why some Chinese were held for as long as two years at the immigration station. In a poem cut into a wall at Angel Island, a Chinese immigrant expressed the feeling of many held there:

Why do I have to languish in this jail?
It is because my country is weak and my family poor.
My parents wait in vain for news;
My wife and child, wrapped in their quilt,
    sigh with loneliness.

Angel Island was a little better than The Shed, as far as conditions went, but not as far as the policies of the Immigration Service were concerned. Again and again, such organizations as the Six Companies, the Chinese government, church groups, and the Angel Island detainees association protested the bad food and miserable living conditions on the island.

After sentiment turned against the Chinese, new immigrants arriving in California ports were sometimes greeted by a hail of stones from riotous citizens. (Bancroft Library)

Detainees on the island rioted in 1919, and then many more times in the 1920s. Because of the protests and riots, conditions improved somewhat during the 1920s, and detainees were held for shorter times. The island was closed in 1940, for by then immigration inspections were finally being held in the countries from which immigrants came, rather than after they had come all the way to America.

But whatever their difficulties in entering, for new Chinese immigrants the Chinese-American community was from the first at the center of life in America. Now we will look at how Chinese life and community developed in the land of the Mountains of Gold.

5

The Early Years In America

In very early Gold Rush days in the West, before all the anti-Chinese bigotry started, the new Chinese-Americans were made welcome and flourished. Here is Judge Nathaniel Bennett of California, welcoming Chinese and other recent immigrants in 1850, at the ceremonies marking the admission of California into statehood:

> Born and reared under different Governments and speaking different tongues, we nevertheless meet here today as brothers . . . . You stand among us in all respects as equals . . . Henceforth we have one country, one hope, one destiny.

And this description of Chinese participation in San Francisco's Washington's Birthday parade in 1852:

> All countries and ages were represented in the ceremonies of the day. Scarcely had the French, Spanish and Hebrew Societies passed from view before some two hundred Celestials [Chinese], or, as their banner termed them, "China Boys of San Francisco," came before the admiring gazer . . . Preceded by their mandarins [leaders] and a band of music, straggling and evidently amused with their position, came this large delegation of our most orderly and industrious citizens.

As we have seen, there were some very small numbers of Chinese in California before the Gold Rush of 1848. One of them was a merchant named Chum Ming, who came to San Francisco in 1847. In 1848, he was one of the first to join the Gold Rush. Like so many of the early miners on the scene, he did find gold, enough to make him write home to China to urge others to come to America.

But not many Chinese immediately came to America. The available records show only a few Chinese coming in 1848, a few hundred more in 1849, and another 400 to 500 in 1850. There may have been more, for the records are far from reliable, but not a great many more. That changed in the early 1850s. Some estimates have it that as many as 25,000 Chinese immigrants had come by the end of 1851, although the immigration records of the time do not show this. The first reliable immigration records show 13,000 Chinese arriving in 1854, at the end of the early California Gold Rush and several years after the height of the craze. Then Chinese immigration dropped to an average of about 5,000 a year until 1868. After that, a much heavier immigration began, averaging about 13,000 a year until 1881. Finally, in 1882 alone, almost 40,000 Chinese immigrants came to America's shores. But then, with the passage of the Chinese Exclusion Act, immigration from China dried up for three-quarters of a century. Only in our own time, starting with immigration law changes during and after World War II, did Chinese immigrants begin to come again in any substantial numbers.

The Six Companies

In China, it had been the scholars, upper class officeholders, and landowners—the "gentry"—who were the most respected Chinese groups. In America, at least in the early years, there were very few Chinese scholars or gentry, so the early arrivals among the merchants took the lead in setting up the tight-knit Chinese-American communities. In San Francisco, Chinese merchants would welcome new arrivals from China. Later, as the Chinese-American community spread out, the practice was initiated in other cities. The welcoming merchants supplied vital necessities. They found the immigrants places to stay, organized means of finding employment and provided Chinese-to-English interpreters. Their aid was vital, indeed, for very few of the arriving Chinese could speak any English at all.

Late in 1849, the San Francisco Chinese merchants formed the first merchant's association. Within the next few years, that association had developed into a group of district associations, much like those back home in China. Within the district associations, there were the smaller clan associations, composed of people with family relationships. By the middle 1850s—only a few years after Chinese-Americans had begun to arrive in any substantial numbers—a whole web of organizations had developed, much like those of the old country.

Before 1911, the Manchus forbade Chinese citizens to cut off their queues—their single, long braids—so those who wished to return home for a visit kept their queues in good shape by weekly trips to their local Chinese barber. (San Francisco Public Library)

The district associations soon developed into a major set of guiding organizations in the new Chinese-American community. As they organized and reorganized over the years, they became the Chinese Consolidated Benevolent Associations (CCBA), known to those outside the Chinese-American community as "the Six Companies."

This kind of a closely knit set of organizations developed in every substantial Chinese-American community in the United States. Later, in the 1880s, all of the Associations together would form a national Chinese Consolidated Benevolent Association. In the decades when the Chinese community was under the worst attack from the forces of bigotry in America this organization would function as the most important Chinese-American defense organization.

In San Francisco, in the early days, the Six Companies did many of the things that the benevolent societies of other immigrant groups did for their members. There were burial societies, credit unions offering loans to members, early immigrant hotels, medical care facilities, and educational organizations. They also provided many of the important employment-getting contacts. The burial societies had special importance, for religious belief caused most immigrants to arrange burial ceremonies in the United States, but to have their bones or ashes returned to China, to their families.

The Chinese-American associations, however, did a great deal more than most other similar ethnic associations. For as anti-Chinese bigotry and activity developed, the early Chinese-American communities were driven inward. Much has been made by some writers of how isolated these Chinese-American communities were, with the Chinese-Americans keeping their own dress and language, and leaving their wives back in China, rather than bringing them to the United States. The Chinese-Americans *were* strongly committed to preserving their culture, traditions, and sense of community in their new land. They had, after all, a long and proud history. But, in truth, the primary reason why the Chinese-Americans kept to themselves was bigotry.

Anti-Chinese actions drove the Chinese away from the American community. Most ethnic groups kept largely to themselves in their early years in America; that was the pattern followed by Irish, Italians, Jews, Poles, and dozens of other ethnic groups. But sooner or later a move out into the wider American community began, and soon enough there was the mixing and partial merging that so makes America what it is. And so it should have been for the Chinese-American community. Here is how the San

Early immigrants who died in America were generally not buried there; instead their bones were often cleansed of flesh in a fire, as here, and the residue returned to China for burial. (Bancroft Library)

Francisco Chinese community put it in an open letter to Governor Bigler of California, in 1852, only a year after the first substantial numbers of Chinese-Americans began to arrive in California.

If the privileges of your laws are open to us, some of us will doubt-less acquire your habits, your language, your ideas, your feelings, your morals, your forms and become citizens of your country. Many have already adopted your religion as their own, and will be good citizens. There are very good Chinamen now in the country; and a better class will, if allowed, come hereafter—men of learning and of wealth, bringing their families with them.

But for the early Chinese-Americans, that wonderful mixing and merging into America did not come. A wave of bigotry came, instead. So the associations took on a pivotal importance. In San Francisco, they eventually became a sort of unofficial local government, even hiring private police to patrol the community and, very importantly, to help protect it from outside attackers. The associations also functioned as a major legal defense organization, taking cases all the way up to the United States Supreme Court in defense of Chinese-American rights.

Not all Chinese-Americans were in the associations. All, however, did share the same strong need for a sense of community. Those not in the associations therefore formed other fraternal orders, many of them the same ones that they had belonged to in China. These orders were called *tongs*, and some tong members, though not all, were also later involved in running whatever criminal activities there were in the Chinese-American community. The most important of these fraternal orders was the same Triad society that had existed in China for hundreds of years. In the United States, it was also known as the Chinese Free Masons.

The Early Chinese-American Community

Sometimes rival tongs—Chinese associations—fought each other for control or influence, as here at Weaverville, near Five Cent Gulch, in June 1854. (From Wide West, *California Historical Society)*

The Chinese-American community that developed in the climate of those times was not able to develop as most other immigrant communities did. One key difference was that the community was mainly male. In many immigrant communities, men have greatly outnumbered women in the early days, with the balance adjusting as more women of the particular ethnic group came to America. But for the Chinese, this did not happen. The reason for this was, first, because the women stayed behind in China, and later because most Chinese women, and men too, were barred from entering the United States.

There were some women in the Chinese-American community. From the start, some merchants' wives and children came to America, and these families developed a full community life.

There were also Chinese-American prostitutes, in some periods numbering well over a thousand. Prostitution is an industry that is always strong where men greatly outnumber women—and in the Chinese-American community men outnumbered women by as much as 25 to 1 in some periods. In 1890, for example, there were about 100,000 men and a little under 4,000 women in the Chinese-American community. These women working as prostitutes were usually sold into what amounted to slavery in China while still in their early teens. They were brought to America by the criminal elements in some of the tongs, and kept in slavery while working as prostitutes in the Unites States. The Chinese-American area of a town or city was, if large enough, generally called Chinatown. The old communities in such cities as San Francisco, New York, Chicago, and Boston are still called Chinatowns, just as there is still an old neighborhood in New York called Little Italy, although most Italians have long since moved elsewhere, as have most Chinese.

In a Chinatown, especially in San Francisco's Chinatown, were to be found all the community kind of things that people far, far from home needed. Here were the Six Companies, with their whole web of finances, services, and communications between America and China. Here were the fraternal orders, where men could meet people from their own families and villages. Here were jobs to be found. Here were the sources of ethnic clothing, food, herbal medicine, Chinese doctors, and all the other special things that each group calls its own and craves. Here were the houses of prostitution and gambling halls, common to every nearly-all-male society. Here, too, was a place of refuge, a place in which to be as safe as possible when there was a need to be safe.

In the early years of largely male Chinese immigrant communities, newcomers would often sleep in dormitories like these, in multitiered bunk beds. (From Frank Leslie's Sunday Magazine, *March 1881; Library of Congress)*

Immigrant Huie Kin remembers San Francisco's Chinatown in the 1860s:

> In the sixties, San Francisco's Chinatown was made up of stores catering to the Chinese only. There was only one store, situated at the corner of Sacramento and Dupont streets, which kept Chinese and Japanese curios for the American trade. Our people were all in their native costume, with queues down their backs, and kept their stores just as they would do in China, with the entire street front open and groceries and vegetables overflowing on the sidewalks. Forty thousand Chinese were then resident in the bay region, and so these stores did a flourishing business. The Oakland Chinatown was a smaller affair, more like a mining camp, with rough board houses on a vacant lot near Broadway and Sixteenth Street. Under the roof of the houses was a shelf . . . reached by a ladder. Here we slept at night, rolled in our blankets much in the manner of Indians.

The Early Miners

For most of the early Chinese-Americans, coming to America meant coming to the "Mountains of Gold." And that is exactly what many thousands of the Chinese-American immigrants did. Thousands of them stayed in San Francisco for only a little while, and then headed for the gold fields. As early as 1852, there were thousands of Chinese-American gold miners. By the late 1850s, there were, according to some estimates, as many as 15,000 Chinese-American gold miners in the West.

In the early years, the California gold fields were very rough, dangerous places. The lure of gold had brought hundreds of thousands of gold-seekers from all over the world, very many of them with little regard for law and order. Nor was gold itself so easy to find and mine. After the first few months, there were far more gold-seekers than high-paying claims. By 1850, the second full year of the Gold Rush, there was a great deal of violence in the gold fields, as miners fought over the shrinking amounts of gold available.

But there was more gold than there seemed to be. Miners seeking big, rich gold strikes often took what they could, fast, and then moved on. For them, their gold claims were often quickly "worked out"—that is, mined so heavily as to make further mining a useless task. The Chinese miners,

On their way to the California gold fields, these Chinese immigrants carried their bedding, food, tools, and other supplies on bags hung from the poles on their shoulders. (From Wide West, 19th century; California Historical Society)

however, were able to patiently and profitably take such "worked out" claims and make them pay. Where the European-American miners worked as individuals or in very small groups, the Chinese-Americans worked in strong, skilled teams. Gold was often found in the beds of running streams and "panned"—that is, dug, then sifted out of those streams. When the panning became poor, most miners moved on. The Chinese-Americans, however, often dammed or diverted the courses of the streams; they then dug and sifted enough out of the remaining dry streambeds to make the mines pay well. They also panned far more patiently and skillfully than other miners, getting a good deal of gold from claims that others had left behind.

Mining in this way, the new Chinese-Americans did not really compete with the other miners. Nor did they want to do so, for they very soon saw that they would be unable to meet violence with violence—and that if they did, they would soon become the victims of unequal laws and armed, anti-Chinese bands of miners.

From very early on, there was a war over who would take the gold in the California gold fields. It was a very real war, too. By the early 1850s, the American miners, many of them recent emigrants from Ireland and

Germany, had driven almost all the Hispanic and French miners from the gold fields, with mob violence backed by whatever passed for law in California at the time. That violence was not, at the start, mainly directed against the Chinese, for they were not direct competitors for the richest claims, but instead were reworking claims no one else wanted. But what was happening in the gold fields and throughout California in those early years was the growth of a particularly vicious and angry kind of racism, directed against anyone whose skin color was anything other than what was then called "white," meaning northern European in origin. Hispanic-Americans, Native Americans, Blacks, and Asians, including the Chinese-Americans, were all lumped together as "colored," and discriminated against. Competition for gold fueled racist sentiment, and ambitious politicians found racism a very useful way to get power.

But much of the racism went far beyond those simple motives. These were still slavery times in the United States, and the long-running argument over slavery that would soon bring on the Civil War was turning violent in such border states as Missouri and Kansas. A large number of

Some Chinese immigrants did not go into the gold fields, but moved directly into service occupations, such as laundries. (From Frank Leslie's Sunday Magazine, March 1881; Library of Congress)

the gold-seekers came from these states. Many also came from the South, where slavery was still an established fact. Putting it all a little differently, bigotry came naturally to many miners and others in pre-war California. Small wonder that bigotry flourished in such fertile soil.

Discrimination Begins

For many of these early Chinese-Americans, the land of the Golden Mountains did turn out to be a land of opportunity. That this should be true is actually quite astonishing. For, almost from the start, this new land also turned out to be a land full of bigotry and discrimination. Writing in 1887, Professor S.E.W. Becker put the situation this way:

> Had the first white immigrants to California found themselves met by a hostile population and hostile laws; had they been beaten in the streets, robbed and plundered by superior numbers; had discriminating taxes [been] enforced against them under the guise of law; had they been refused citizenship and their children admission to the public schools and all of them police protection; the chances are they would not have fallen in love with the people, the country, the religions, or the laws.

In 1850, only a year after the Gold Rush, the California legislature passed a huge, $20-a-month Foreign Miners License Tax, aimed at driving the many thousands of Hispanic miners from the gold fields. Many did leave, and so did many of the small number of Chinese miners, going back to San Francisco or staying on in non-mining jobs in the gold fields. This tax was not initially aimed at the Chinese miners, but it did set a pattern for much of what was to follow.

This early tax was repealed in 1851 and replaced by a more realistic $3-a-month tax, later to become a $4-a-month tax. For 18 years, until the tax was declared unconstitutional by the United States Supreme Court, that tax supplied huge amounts of money to California's county treasuries. Most of it was paid by the "foreign" Chinese-American miners. None of it was paid back after the law was declared unconstitutional.

Nor could Chinese-Americans do anything but remain"foreigners" in the eyes of California law. For in California they were denied the right to become American citizens, though they could become citizens in other

CHINESE MINERS.

Chinese miners in the California gold fields lived a rough life in primitive tents, as did most other prospectors. (From Harpers Weekly, October 3, 1857; Library of Congress)

parts of the country. The California constitution of 1849 limited the right to vote to "white male citizens of the United States." That limit was used as justification for denying Chinese-American Californians citizenship, as well. This was a matter of simple racism, for the Chinese-Americans were treated then as "colored" people, and discriminated against just as were the Blacks and Native Americans of the time.

The California courts made that abundantly clear. In 1854, the California Supreme Court ruled that Chinese-Americans, along with "Indians" and Blacks, could not give testimony in the state courts. That remained the law for 19 years, until 1873, and guaranteed unequal treatment before the law for Chinese-Americans. A gold mining claim could be stolen, and the courts would not even listen to the Chinese-American from whom it was stolen. A contract could be ignored, or a claim for damages made, and the Chinese-American harmed could not even come into court to testify as to that harm. There was more—for example, it was only years later that a whole series of state laws aimed at barring admission to the country were declared unconstitutional by the United States Supreme Court.

One key effect of this whole discriminatory legal system was to make it very easy to take lawless action against Chinese-Americans. Much of the violence came later, but even in the early years there were many instances of anti-Chinese mob violence in the gold fields, and instances in San Francisco, as well.

The net effect of this whole system of official and unofficial discrimination was to make it impossible for the new Chinese-Americans to take what otherwise would have been their normal place in American society. There were "white" Americans who held out the hand of friendship, but they were so few and far between that they made no real dent in the racism of the day. To a large extent, after the first few years, the early Chinese-Americans were on their own in a hostile land.

In *Roughing It* (1872), Mark Twain described the situation very clearly:

A disorderly Chinaman is rare, and a lazy one does not exist. So long as a Chinaman has strength to use his hands he needs no support from anybody; white men often complain of want of work, but a Chinaman offers no such complaint; he always manages to find something to do. He is a great convenience to everybody—even to the worst class of white men, for he bears the most of their sins, suffering fines for their petty thefts, imprisonment for their robberies, and death for their murders. Any white man can swear a Chinaman's life away in the courts, but no Chinaman can testify against a white man. Ours is the "land of the free"—nobody denies that—nobody challenges it. (Maybe it is because we won't let other people testify.) As I write, news comes that in broad daylight in San Francisco, some boys have stoned an inoffensive Chinaman to death, and that although a large crowd witnessed the shameful deed, no one interfered.

Yet, with all the discrimination, the new Chinese-American played a very large role in the building of the American West, and built a strong, early Chinese-American community.

6

Building the West

In the half century after the Gold Rush, Chinese-Americans made enormous contributions to the building of the American West, even though they faced discrimination every step of the way. They extracted gold and other minerals from the earth, developed the huge, rich farmlands of central and northern California, fished the seas off the West Coast, and were active in dozens of other vital occupations throughout the West. And they built a big section of the first transcontinental railroad, joining the coasts together and making possible the American nation as we know it today.

Building the Railroads

Many historians and writers have called attention to one of the most popular pictures found in our history books. It is a picture of the completion of the first transcontinental railroad, at Promontory Point, Utah, on May 10, 1869. This scene is often described as the driving of the Golden Spike, the last spike linking the Union Pacific and Central Pacific railroads. The Union Pacific had come a long way from Omaha, Nebraska, all the way west across the plains of mid-America. The Central Pacific had come a long, even harder way, east from Sacramento across some of the most difficult mountain ranges in the world. The work crews of the Union Pacific were composed mostly of recent Irish-American immigrants. The work crews of the central Pacific were mostly recent Chinese-American immigrants.

But there are no Chinese-Americans in this most famous picture! Here, as throughout the West, the Chinese became invisible, their great contributions hidden even in our history books.

Yet, they did build the railroad. Actually, if not for them, the Central Pacific part of the road might not have been built at all in those years.

In 1862, during the Civil War, Congress authorized the building of the first transcontinental railroad, which was designed to link the Atlantic and Pacific, making the United States a single, completely unified continental power. Work started on the railroad and continued in 1863 and 1864, but in the West little progress was being made. The work was hard, and the pay was nothing like what might be made in the new gold and silver fields in the Northwest, Nevada, and the Rockies. Thousands of men were hired by the Central Pacific, but fewer than half actually went to work on the railroad for more than a few days. Charles Crocker, one of the four main investors in the railroad, suggested that Chinese laborers be brought in to work on the project. His suggestion was at first not taken seriously. Although Chinese-Americans had by then been successful miners for many years, the railroad people generally thought that they were too small and weak for the hard work involved. That mistaken idea was soon put to rest, when the Chinese-American work crews proved entirely able to master the work. They were, in fact, just as good at it as the mainly Irish-American crews building the railroad from the East.

Soon, the successful Chinese-American railroad builders were known as "Crocker's pets," and were going to work on the railroad by the thousands. E.B. Crocker described what the railroad's founders soon learned about the Chinese railroad builders:

> A large part of our forces are Chinese, and they prove nearly equal to white men, in the amount of labor they perform, and are far more reliable. No danger of strikes among them. We are training them to all kinds of labor, blasting, driving horses, handling rock, as well as the pick and shovel. . . . We want to get a body of 2,500 trained laborers, and keep them steadily at work until the road is built clear across the continent.

At the height of the work, estimates are that 10,000 Chinese-Americans worked as builders of that first transcontinental railroad. They worked in tremendous heat and bitter cold. They tunneled through mountains, bridged huge streams and canyons, and took the railroad over the Sierra Nevada and Rocky Mountains.

Later, after completion of the railroad, they went on to become the main builders of the Southern Pacific railroad and the Northwest Pacific railroad, extending the vitally important railroad network throughout the West.

Chinese immigrant workers provided much of the labor needed to build tracks and trestles through the difficult Sierra Nevada Mountains of California. (Southern Pacific Transportation Company)

Laborers of Chinese and European descent worked together in building the last mile of the transcontinental railroad. (By A.H. Waud, Harper's Weekly, May 29, 1869; Library of Congress)

Leland Stanford, president of the Central Pacific Railroad, and later founder of Stanford University, summed up the Chinese contribution to the building of the railroad:

> As a class, they are quiet, peaceable, patient, industrious, and economical. More prudent and economical, they are contented with less wages. We find them organized for mutual aid and assistance. Without them, it would be impossible to complete the western portion of this great national enterprise within the time required by the Act of Congress.

Farming the Land

The Chinese have for thousands of years been among the most productive farmers in the world. In America, they were soon able to turn their old farming skills into valuable occupations.

Even before completion of the transcontinental railroad, Chinese Californians were employed to bring in the state's large wheat harvest. Without them, it would probably have been impossible or at least very difficult to do so. Just as there was a great shortage of workers for railroad building, so too was there a great shortage of farm labor. The Chinese-Americans were in those years a source of absolutely necessary harvest labor, much as the West's mainly Hispanic farm workers are today.

Once the railroad was completed, and the rest of the West's railroad network began to be set in place, many new markets were opened up for the distribution of California fruits and vegetables. The California farmers continued to plant wheat, but now also grew large quantities of fruits, vegetables, and flowers. Pears, apples, plums, sugar beets, peanuts, chrysanthemums, peas, and a great deal more were grown and sold all over the country.

For the last few decades of the 19th century, it was the Chinese-Americans who made the huge expansion of California farming possible. Then, as now, California farms tended to be large, with the land held by a relatively small number of farmers. Then, as now, the crops required a great deal of labor to produce, rather than being easy to tend and harvest with machines.

The Chinese-Americans did the job, from planting right through to harvesting. Some also went into business on their own, although discriminatory California law barred them from owning land. Most continued to work as farmhands, but some were able to make profit-sharing agreements with their employers. Others rented land and put it to various uses. Some planted vegetable-growing "truck" gardens and sold their produce in nearby towns and cities. Some used their rented land to raise such widely diverse crops as strawberries, peanuts, and celery. Still others rented and worked existing orchards, producing and selling such fruits as apples, pears, and plums.

The Chinese-Americans who came to California were from the Pearl River delta, an area much like the flooded San Joaquin and Sacramento river deltas of northern and central California. Living in the Pearl River delta Chinese were highly skilled in reclaiming land from the rivers and the sea.

In California, Chinese-American farmers had an opportunity to put their valuable skills to work once again. Starting in the 1860s, thousands of Chinese-Americans were employed in highly skilled land reclamation

Chinese farmers were so productive that railroads printed advertisements in Chinese to persuade them to ship their produce by rail. (California Historical Society)

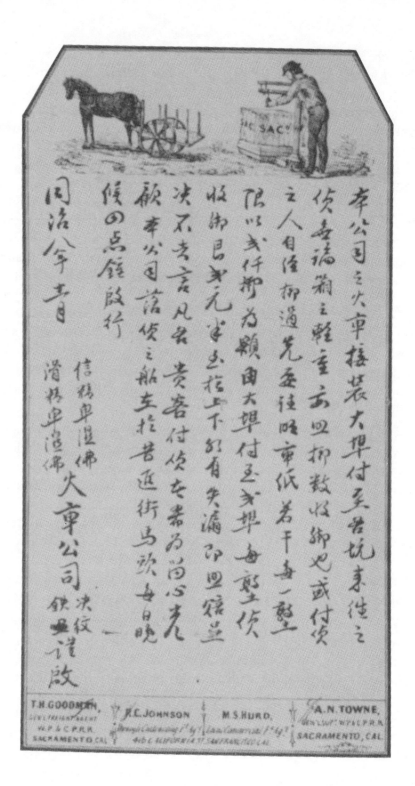

crews. By 1877, they had succeeded in creating a full five million acres of valuable land—today some of the most valuable farmland in the world—from what had been nearly worthless flooded land. These were the "tule reed lands," which are now tremendously fertile farming valleys.

The Chinese created their dams and drainage devices mainly by hand. Later, machines took over. Today, many of the huge, machine-made levees and drainage canals of northern and central California still have at their centers the original Chinese walls and canals.

Chinese-Americans also made up most of the early labor force in California's grape, raisin, and wine industry. From the early 1860s through the 1880s, they handled every aspect of the work involved, including the cutting of the huge storage tunnels required by the new wineries.

Some of these early Chinese-American farmers were also developers of new products and processes. The popular Bing cherry is named after its developer, Ah Bing. The great horticulturist Luey Gim Gong developed many new strains of fruit, his most notable being the hardy, frost-resistant strain of orange now known as the Florida orange.

Had there been less discrimination in the West, and especially in California, there is little doubt that skilled Chinese-American farmers would have settled in and developed farms and farming communities of their own, much as Scandinavians did in the upper Midwest and Germans in Pennsylvania. But it was not to be.

In the 1870s and 1880s, a very strong anti-Chinese movement built up throughout the West. In California, where Dennis Kearney's anti-Chinese, anti-foreigner Workingmen's Party grew very strong, hard times in the 1870s made it easy to brand the Chinese as foreigners who were taking "American" jobs and working for next to nothing. That this was not true had nothing to do with the success of the anti-Chinese campaign. These anti-Chinese movements greatly encouraged the passage of the national Chinese Exclusion Act of 1882 and other anti-Chinese legislation.

During the 1880s, as part of the widespread bigotry of the time, there were anti-Chinese riots in many of California's small farming towns. These riots were common in mining towns and larger cities throughout the West.

The Workingman's Party of California (W.P.C.) presented a slate of candidates in 1878 under the slogan "The Chinese Must Go!"—and got enough votes to elect several of them. (California State Library)

The United States suffered a major depression in 1893. California was hit hard, with massive unemployment and a large number of bank and other business failures. Unemployed whites demanding Chinese-American farming jobs rioted in many California towns and cities, from Fresno and the San Joaquin valley in the north all the way south to the orange-growing country. Everywhere it was the same. Chinese-American farm workers were forced off the land by armed rioters, who often also beat and robbed them and burned down their homes. In the end, the long years of bigotry and anti-Chinese riots and massacres forced most Chinese-Americans off the land.

Only a few Chinese-American farmers remained on the land in California. As late as the 1920s, there were still pockets of the original Chinese-American farmers in California, especially in the few areas that had put up some resistance to anti-Chinese movements and riots. Ironically, after the Chinese-Americans were forced off the land, all that happened was that a succession of other immigrants were brought in by the big growers. After the Chinese-Americans came Japanese, other East Asians, and Mexicans, each in turn discriminated against and at the same time accused of taking "American" jobs—jobs that no one else would actually take.

Chinese farmers, like this one in Sacramento, were driven off the farms of California and back into the urban Chinatowns, where they were under the protection of the ethnic associations, such as the Chinese Benevolent Association. (By Dorothea Lange, Library of Congress)

A very small number of Chinese farmers had been employed elsewhere in the country as contract farm laborers, notably in such southern states as Louisiana, Mississippi, and Arkansas. They were not slave or "coolie" laborers, but worked under labor contracts that specified wages, hours, and working conditions for periods of up to five years. But very few stayed there—nor could they be forced to stay by their employers under American law. Most chose to leave the southern farms. Some of these Chinese-Americans moved into such cities as New Orleans, while others eventually made their way west.

A Fishing People

The people of the Pearl River delta had always lived close to the sea, and many had made their livings from the sea. They were mainly a farming people, but they were also a fishing people. It was therefore quite natural that many of them would turn to fishing and other sea-related work in America.

By the 1850s, a strong Chinese-American fishing trade had developed off the California coast. Working out of fleets of small boats—sampans—fishers caught a wide variety of fish, including herring, sole, smelt, cod, sturgeon, and shark, which was and is a staple in Chinese cooking. Working out of larger boats—junks—they caught larger fish, such as barracuda. They fished the seas and bays for shrimp and other shellfish, fished the rivers for salmon, gathered clams and abalone, and harvested the seaweed, another staple in Chinese cooking.

By the 1880s, Chinese-Americans were fishing off the entire West Coast, between the Canadian and the Mexican borders. Many young men had also gone to work in the salmon canneries of the Northwest. Later, many more went to work in the Alaska canneries; these were a source of work as late as the 1930s, long after almost all Chinese-Americans were forced out of the fishing industry.

In this industry, that forcing out was not accomplished mainly by anti-Chinese rioting, as had happened in farming. Here, it was a matter of steady pressure, with a long stream of discriminatory laws and taxes accompanied by many violent incidents. There were special fishing taxes levied on "foreigners"; these were aimed at the Chinese-Americans, who were barred by law from becoming citizens. There were denials of fishing

licenses, restrictions on the use of Chinese-style nets, the barring of junks from California waters, and a great deal more. As a result, most Chinese-Americans were driven out of the fishing industry.

Other Occupations

A general pattern of discrimination against Chinese-American businesses made money for expansion very hard to raise. There was also a long, bitter anti-Chinese campaign waged by the main Western trade unions that made it impossible for most Chinese-American workers to take their place as a part of the American trade union movement.

However, in such small Western industries as cigar-making, the clothing trades, and the boot and shoe industries, Chinese businesspeople and

Chinese immigrants worked in many of the small industries of the West, such as shoemaking, before the larger, more efficient industries of the East took over. (Library of Congress)

industrial workers were able to work hard and successfully to develop profitable businesses. There was no successful campaign to drive Chinese-Americans from these light industries, as had occurred in mining, farming, and fishing. Partly, that was because many of these Chinese-American businesses were located in and near the Chinatown communities. Also, some of these businesses and jobs were low-paying and not terribly profitable. Easterners pouring into the West in search of easy riches were not attracted to such jobs.

In China, skilled workers had for centuries developed their own organizations, or guilds. In the United States, Chinese workers also formed guilds, but these were run in essentially the same way as American trade unions, from which Chinese were barred. They negotiated with employers for better wages and working conditions and went on strike when necessary. There were Chinese-American worker guilds in the cigar industry, in the clothing industry, and in the boot and shoe industry, among others.

Leaders of organized labor in those years often called Chinese workers "strikebreakers." And some employers did attempt to use them as strikebreakers, although hardly ever with success. In the early 1870s, a small force of Chinese-American shoe workers, numbering less than 100, were taken all the way to North Adams, Massachusetts, to break a strike. No one told them why they had been brought in, and only one of them spoke a small amount of English. But instead of attacking the Chinese, the local people took them in, helped them to learn English, and found them better jobs. Some of the labor leaders of the time used this as an example of Chinese strikebreaking. In fact, it was an example of how easy it would have been to bring Chinese-Americans into the American labor movement, but for the bigotry of the time.

In such light industries, where many small companies were owned by Chinese-American businesspeople, Chinese-American workers and their

Within the many Chinatowns across the country were restaurants, like this one in San Francisco, serving the ethnic community; only later did such restaurants become attractive to the general population. (Bancroft Library)

guilds flourished. But as American industry began to use more and bigger machines, Eastern competition became difficult to meet. In the cigar industry, Eastern factories—larger and more expensive to build—began producing their rolled tobacco more cheaply by the mid-1880s. At the same time, cigar smoking was in decline, as machine-produced cigarettes began to gain in popularity. By the turn of the century, San Francisco's 6,000 to 7,000 cigar workers, most of them Chinese-Americans, had dwindled down to only a hundred strong. In the garment trades, woolen mills, and shoe industry, much the same happened. These small Western industries were unable to compete against the developing, large Eastern factories, and most went out of business.

There were, however, some kinds of business which Chinese-Americans continued to run successfully. From the earliest days in San

After being driven from land and sea, many Chinese-Americans found work as servants, like these pictured in Helena's Social Supremacy. (Montana Historical Society)

HELENA'S CORRECT STANDARDS OF LIVING.

Francisco and in the gold fields, there had been Chinese restaurants, Chinese hand laundries, Chinese domestic workers, and a wide variety of merchants inside the Chinese-American communities. All these occupations continued to survive and grow, as the population of the West increased, and as Chinese-American communities grew in other parts of the country. These were the basic occupations that were to sustain the community through the difficult times ahead.

7

Hard Times

*To an American death is preferable to a
life on a par with the Chinaman . . .
Treason is better than to labor beside a
Chinese slave . . . The people are about
to take their own affairs into their own
hands and they will not be stayed either
by "Citizen Vigilantes," state militia,
nor United States troops.*

*Manifesto of Workingmen's Party
California, October 17, 1876*

*Large gatherings of the idle and
irresponsible element of the population of this city are nightly addressed
in the open streets by speakers who
use the most violent, inflammatory
and incendiary language, threatening
in plainest terms to burn and pillage
the Chinese quarter and kill our
people unless, at their bidding, we
leave this "free republic." . . . We
appeal to you, the Mayor and Chief
Magistrate of this Municipality, to
protect us to the full extent of your
power in all our peaceful, constitu-
tional, and treaty rights . . . . We
should also regret to have the good
name of this Christian civilization*

81

*tarnished by the riotous proceedings of
its own citizens against the "Chinese
heathen."*

*Appeal of the Chinese Six Companies
San Francisco, November 3, 1876*

During the Los Angeles anti-Chinese riot of 1871, 21 Chinese-Americans were murdered, and much of the Chinese-American community was destroyed.

On July 23, 1877, in San Francisco, an anti-Chinese street meeting of an estimated 10,000 people developed into a three-day-long anti-Chinese riot. Chinese-Americans were attacked throughout the city and scores of their businesses were burned down, while rioters fought the police. Finally, units of the United States Army and Navy, together with the city's Vigilance Committee, restored order.

In 1878, the whole Chinese-American population of Truckee, California—about 1,000 people in all—were driven out of the town by an anti-Chinese mob.

In 1880, the Denver, Colorado, anti-Chinese riots resulted in one murder of a Chinese-American, many injuries, and much damage to the community.

In 1885, in Rock Springs, Wyoming, 28 Chinese-Americans were murdered during an anti-Chinese riot.

The above are only five instances of the hundreds of attacks in those years aimed at driving Chinese-Americans out of the West. What began to happen in the 1870s, and kept on happening all during the rest of the 19th century and beyond, was that the isolated anti-Chinese acts and local laws of the early years became a pattern of discrimination.

In California and throughout the West, a series of politicians and labor leaders used bigotry to advance their careers. One of the worst of these was Dennis Kearney, founder of the Workingmen's Party, whose manifesto is quoted at the beginning of this chapter. But he had a great deal of company, including the founder of the American Federation of Labor, Samuel Gompers, whose anti-Chinese work, *Meat and Rice*, published in 1901, greatly helped the anti-Chinese, anti-foreigner movements of the time. Later, during the anti-foreign hysteria of the 1920s, the same kind of

Anti-Chinese riots and massacres, like this one in Colorado, occurred throughout the West in the 1880s. (Colorado Historical Society)

views and movements would be used to close the Golden Door to emigrants from southern and eastern Europe.

Exclusion

When it becomes strong enough, hysteria fanned by self-serving politicians can lead to national laws. And that is what happened to the early Chinese-Americans. For many years, the United States Supreme Court had struck down anti-Chinese law after anti-Chinese law passed by the California state legislature. Finally, though, anti-Chinese hysteria grew so strong that in 1880 the United States government renegotiated the Burlingame treaty with China. This was the key treaty the Supreme Court had used to strike down many anti-Chinese laws and practices. After that, the United States Congress passed a series of anti-Chinese laws that closed the door to almost all Chinese immigration for over half a century.

The result of all the anti-Chinese hysteria, anti-Chinese attacks, and anti-Chinese laws was the coming of an even harder time for Chinese-Americans. They had been driven off the farmland they had themselves created out of worthless swampland. They had been driven out of the mines and off the sea. They had been murdered and burnt out. They had been excluded from citizenship, from the courts, and finally from immigrating to or even returning to the United States. Chinese-American Chan Kiu Sing, writing in 1904, commented bitterly: "They call it exclusion; but it is not exclusion, it is extermination."

Tens of thousands of Chinese-Americans simply gave up on America and went back home to China. In 1890, there were a little over 100,000 Chinese-Americans. By 1920, there were only about half that number. Some Chinese-Americans had grown old and died or gone back to China in their later years. But many left because of discrimination and did not come back.

Staying On

The surprising thing is that so many of the early Chinese-Americans stayed during those very hard years, and that some Chinese still wanted to come to America. Those who did come tended to go into service occupations, usually as small businesspeople running what became the "traditional" Chinese-American laundries and Chinese restaurants. Others became domestic workers, such as cooks and gardeners. These had been the occupations of many Chinese-Americans before the very bad years. Now they became the occupations of the great majority, for these were jobs which other Americans did not really want. A few thousand still worked in farming, mainly in the small pockets of resistance that had survived the main driving from the land in California. A few thousand also worked in light industry. But the majority of those Chinese-Americans who stayed in America drew inward, into a much smaller remaining number of Chinatowns, and into those small businesses and service occupations least likely to be attacked.

During the 1870s, as physical attacks on Chinese communities grew throughout the West, San Francisco's Chinatown became very much like a fortress under siege. The Six Companies hired special non-Chinese police, not to bring order in Chinatown but to repel anti-Chinese mobs. These mobs had threatened to overrun and burn out the area on several occasions, especially at the height of the anti-Chinese riots of 1877. Many Chinese-American organizations armed themselves, and prepared to fight as necessary should Chinatown be invaded. The Los Angeles Chinatown massacre of 1871 could easily have been repeated on a much larger scale if the mobs had won in San Francisco.

In the troubled times when anti-Chinese discrimination ran strong, the officials of San Francisco's Six Companies, shown here, organized for the defense of the immigrant community. (By Louis J. Stellman, California State Library)

As the Chinese-American community was driven inward, the San Francisco community did become a kind of fortress. By the late 1880s, there were about 30,000 Chinese-Americans crammed into the 12-square-block area that was then San Francisco's Chinatown. The prestige of the Six Companies was low, for the leaders of the community had failed to stop the tide of hysteria and exclusion. The community was poor, with so many having been driven from their occupations. The criminal elements in the tongs were strong, for the whole community was in desperate condition; Chinatown was turning into a city slum while San Francisco boomed all around it. Prostitution, drugs, and gambling all flourished, as Chinese criminals worked with corrupt police and city officials for mutual profit. Some of the tongs fought each other for control, bringing danger to Chinatown residents and providing ammunition for bigots outside the community.

Through it all there were also some Westerners who would not join in the anti-Chinese hysteria. In 1877, it was San Francisco's Vigilance Committee, with its 5,000-strong "Pickax Brigade" that did the most to stop the mob attacking the Chinese community. In Chinatown, such organizations as the Presbyterian Mission, led by Donaldina Cameron, fought to help Chinese slave-prostitutes and to decrease the corruption that made them slaves. Out in the country, there were a small number of farming communities that just would not give way to the hysteria. Here, local law enforcement officials, backed by their communities, did not let mobs drive the Chinese-Americans from the land.

Resisting Exclusion

For 61 years, from 1882 to 1943, Chinese-Americans and new emigrants from China resisted exclusion in every legal and illegal way they could. The Six Companies fought hundreds of cases in the courts, some of them all the way to the Supreme Court, often with the aim of reuniting families broken apart by exclusion. Many of the cases turned on the question of citizenship, for until the immigration law of 1924, the Chinese children of American citizens could legally come to the United States. Many other cases involved the question of the occupation of Chinese-Americans, for until the Supreme Court ruled otherwise in the 1920s, the non-citizen wives and children of Chinese merchants could legally come to the United States, while other Chinese non-citizens could not.

Sometimes great tragedies have unexpected results. One great tragedy, the San Francisco earthquake of 1906, had the unexpected result of making it very hard to prove that Chinese-Americans claiming citizenship were *not* citizens. Anyone born in the United States was a citizen by birthright. But, along with most of the city, the immigration records burned. As a direct result, thousands of Chinese-Americans claimed citizenship, backing their claims with imaginary personal histories and sometimes with false papers. Suddenly, many single men who could not possibly have been born in the United States, if only because of the scarcity of Chinese-American women, became citizens by birthright. Some of those who so claimed citizenship certainly were American citizens by birth, but many were not. It was impossible to prove the matter either way. The results were a large number of court cases and a good many citizenships that otherwise might not have been.

Those who wanted to bring their families to America also very often claimed merchant status, for merchants and their families were not excluded "laborers" and could be admitted to the United States—though often after long detention and questioning at The Shed or at Angel Island. Some of those claiming merchant status went into business with their families in mind. Oddly enough, the very driving of the Chinese-American community off the land and sea and out of the mines also drove many into small businesses of their own. As workers for others, they could not bring in their families; as merchants, they could.

One result of the resistance to exclusion was the creation of "paper sons." It worked this way: A Chinese-American returning the United States after a visit to China would report the birth of a son while in China, and sometimes also the birth of a son six or seven months after his return to the United States. Such children—if they had really existed—would be American citizens, with citizenship "deriving" from their father. Later, people claiming to be these sons would claim their right to be admitted as American citizens, with their "fathers" stating that these were, indeed, their children. Several thousand Chinese immigrants gained admission to the United States as "paper sons."

But this kind of resistance to exclusion often carried lifelong hazards, for it was used in what came to be known as the "slot racket." The "slot" was those years of the "father's" life in which the "sons" were said to have been born. These claimed citizenships were frequently sold for profit, and often by the criminal elements in the Chinese and Chinese-American communities. When that happened, these "fathers" and "sons" were open to blackmail for the rest of their lives. The exposure of such false claims would certainly lead to deportation, often after the "sons" had built whole lives and families in America. Chinese immigrants generally understood that, but did it anyway, for otherwise many would not have been able to come to America at all.

There was also a good deal of illegal border-crossing by Chinese immigrants in those years. Most "illegals" came across the Mexican border, just as other "illegals" have come before and since. Others came across illegally from Canada. But for those coming in this way to America, life was often very difficult, even with false papers. In those years, the Immigration Service conducted many raids into Chinese-American communities, and discovery meant deportation. Here, too, there was a great deal of opportunity for blackmail. Many of the people who organized such border crossings were criminals who in turn practiced blackmail for decades afterward.

In his mid-80s in 1913, Sam Lee—mayor of one of America's many Chinatowns—had given up his queue and Asian-style dress. (Copyright Washington Post; reprinted by permission of the D.C. Public Library)

As this cartoon indicates, after the United States virtually closed down emigration from China, some Chinese immigrants tried to enter through British Columbia, in western Canada. (Bancroft Library)

The Community Goes On

Even through the hardest times, the Chinese-American community managed to go on. It was certainly very badly hurt. Many left the United States and many more retreated into San Francisco's Chinatown to weather the storm of anti-Chinese hysteria and exclusion. But it survived, developing a strong, vital life of its own, and eventually beginning to grow and spread out once again as the storm grew less intense.

Even in the worst of times, there were people in the community who were moving ahead. Some of them ran newspapers that greatly influenced the development of the Chinese-American community. There had been Chinese-American newspapers in the very early days, notably San Francisco's Chinese-language *Golden Hill News*, first published in 1854. There were other Chinese-language newspapers in that period as well, but none lasted very long.

The first long-lasting and influential Chinese-American newspaper was San Francisco's *Chinese World*, published in both Chinese and English, from 1891 through 1969. The second was Dr. Ng Poon-Chew's *China-*

West Daily, first published in San Francisco in 1900, which lasted until 1951. This newspaper had great influence, as from the start it attacked the old Manchu customs and fought for education and better integration into American society. As the century developed, it had many willing listeners.

A third major newspaper was the *Young China Morning Paper*, which backed the revolutionary activity of Sun Yat-sen in China, activity that was to lead to the revolution of 1911. That revolution overthrew the Manchus, and established the Chinese Republic. Sun Yat-sen was to become the "father" of the Chinese Republic, much as was George Washington for the United States.

The early Chinese-Americans had brought their traditional beliefs with them from China. These included a continuing belief in the wisdom of Confucius and strong respect (amounting to worship) for their ancestors. That is why it was so very important to have some remains shipped back to China for burial, even when there was actual burial in the United States. Many Chinese-Americans also continued to practice Buddhism or Taoism. Very often, a single person might believe in parts of all three of these great Chinese systems of belief.

A few Chinese-Americans had adopted Christianity, usually some form of Protestantism, while still in China, where there was much Christian missionary work. There was also a good deal of Christian missionary work in the new Chinese-American communities. But the Christian missionaries had only modest success, and Christianity never achieved a dominant position in the Chinese-American community. Perhaps as much as 20% of the community eventually adopted some kind of Christian faith, mostly Protestant, while some became Catholics. In the homeland, there were and are a small number of Chinese Jews, and a rather substantial number of Chinese Moslems, mostly in East Central Asia. But there is no record of any substantial number of Chinese-American Jews or Moslems.

No religious organization, whether traditional Chinese or Christian, has ever had a very strong position in the Chinese-American community. There has been nothing, for example, like the position of the main religious organizations in the Jewish community, or of the Catholic Church in the Irish-American community. Religion has played a strong role in many individual Chinese-American lives, but the main organizations of the community have been secular, rather than religious.

During the 1890s, while many Chinese-Americans were leaving for China because of discrimination in America, others migrated to other

This man, still wearing the queue that was his passport to visit his homeland, was the first Chinese telephone operator in San Francisco's Chinatown. (Library of Congress)

parts of the United States. In such northern cities as New York, Boston, and Chicago, the small Chinese populations doubled and tripled. The new arrivals tended to move into the same kind of laundry, restaurant, and service occupations that they had moved into in the West. In the South, the new Chinese-American migrants joined those who had come years before as contract laborers and stayed on to run businesses, mainly as grocery store owners and workers, but also to run restaurant businesses in the cities.

In San Francisco itself, the great earthquake of 1906 destroyed most of the city, and changed a great deal. To the great majority of San Franciscans, building a new San Francisco literally on the ashes of the old also meant sweeping away the corruption of the old city. Reform came, and with it an attack on criminal elements throughout the city, including those in the Chinese-American community.

The earthquake also brought an opportunity to build a new Chinatown, for the old one was almost entirely destroyed by the earthquake and the fire that followed. That was done, and right on the location of the old Chinatown. The new community to emerge in the years that followed would be quite different from the old, and more consciously American.

8

The Chinese-Hawaiian-Americans

In Hawaii, it all worked out quite differently. There was an early Chinese migration to the islands, much of it from the same South China areas that sent Chinese to the United States, and at much the same time. There was similar early experience on the land. There was anti-Chinese feeling, sometimes verging on hysteria, and much of it imported from the American mainland. And there was a period of exclusion, carried over from the American laws after Hawaii was annexed by the United States. But there was never the kind of hysteria that existed on the mainland, complete with massacres and mass expulsions from land, sea, and mines. The Chinese-Americans of Hawaii were never driven inward into their own communities. The process of mixing and partial assimilation took place in Hawaii far sooner that it did on the mainland, and with far less pain and discrimination. There certainly was discrimination; but the situation of Chinese-Americans in Hawaii was not so bad as to stop or seriously slow the flow of Chinese-Hawaiian immigrants and their children into the Hawaiian mainstream.

The Land of the Sandalwood Mountains

It took only about 40 years, from the 1790s to the 1830s, for Hawaii's sandalwood forests to be used up by Western traders sailing to Canton. That trade had started only a few years after Britain's Captain Cook discovered the islands in 1788, naming them the Sandwich Islands. By the time the trade in sandalwood had been ended, only a few Chinese had visited the islands, some as sailors and a few as the earliest Chinese-Hawaiian settlers. Yet the trade gave Hawaii the name it was to carry in China—the Land of the Sandalwood Mountains (Tan Heung Shan).

The main Chinese migration to Hawaii took place during the second half of the 19th century. During this period over 50,000 Chinese came to the Land of the Sandalwood Mountains, with tens of thousands of them staying to build Hawaii's Chinese-American community.

But the early Chinese migration was quite small, no more than a few hundred Chinese. Almost all of them were merchants or skilled craftspeople from Kwangtung. Among this group were storekeepers, carpenters, some cooks and waiters, and a few farmers. Like many of the American planters who began to come to the islands in the 1830s, some of these early Chinese-Hawaiian farmers planted sugar cane, rice, and coffee.

From the 1820s on, American Christian missionaries and planters came to the islands in increasing numbers. American influence grew steadily over the next 75 years, resulting in United States annexation in 1898 of what had become the independent republic of Hawaii in 1894. What also happened during that first half century of foreign settlement in Hawaii was the importation of epidemic diseases that greatly cut the Polynesian population of the islands. Earlier, when the Europeans had come to the Americas after Columbus, the native populations were attacked by the diseases the Europeans brought with them. The Europeans had built up resistance to these diseases over thousands of years, but the Native Americans had not. As a result they died by the hundreds of thousands and perhaps millions. In Hawaii, during the 19th century, the same thing happened. There were an estimated 225,000 Hawaiians when Captain Cook came in 1788. By 1875, there were only about 50,000 left. There had been some intermarriage with other people by then, but by far the main cause of the decline was the impact of the new diseases, including both cholera and bubonic plague. This created the need that brought the Chinese workers to Hawaii.

The Contract Laborers

In Hawaii, starting in the 1850s, a contract labor system developed. Both Chinese and American planters imported Chinese laborers to work their growing plantations. Chinese rice planters, so used to growing rice successfully in their native Kwangtung, soon came to dominate the rice trade. The American planters concentrated on sugar cane and coffee, and later on pineapples, as well. The Chinese planters also grew sugar cane and coffee, but later tended to move into other trading occupations.

Chinese were welcomed and even recruited to work on Hawaiian plantations. Here, some are harvesting sugar cane in about 1895, long after they had become unwelcome in the mainland United States. (Hawaii State Archives)

Both Chinese-Hawaiians and American-Hawaiians in these early years imported small numbers of Chinese contract laborers. The early immigrant laborers were not from Kwangtung, sailing out of Hong Kong and Macao. Instead, they were from Fukien sailing out of Amoy, farther north on the Chinese coast. They were mostly Hakkas, one of the non-Han Chinese minorities, and a very different people from the Kwangtungese. Indeed, the two groups' languages were so different that they found it easiest to speak with each other in Hawaiian, rather than Chinese. Later, when far larger numbers of Chinese immigrants came to Hawaii, almost all were from Kwangtung, as were most of the Chinese who went to the American mainland.

As mainland American markets grew, especially for sugar and rice, so did the demand for plantation workers. Until the mid-1870s, native Hawaiians continued to supply the majority of the plantation workers. But their population continued to decline, and the demand for workers kept increasing. Then, in 1875, Hawaii and the United States signed a Reciprocity Treaty, giving the products of each country favored treatment in the other country. The American demand for Hawaiian sugar, rice, and later pineapples increased by leaps and bounds, and with it grew the importation of Chinese plantation labor into Hawaii. From 1852 to 1875, Chinese arrivals in Hawaii had averaged only a little more than 100 a year. But from 1876 to 1899, Chinese arrivals in Hawaii averaged well over 2,000 a year.

An estimated two-thirds of all the Chinese coming to Hawaii in those years went to work on the sugar and rice plantations, on three- to five-year contracts. A few hundred of them stayed on the plantations for the rest of their working lives, but the vast majority left as soon as possible. They either bought out their contracts early with money borrowed from other Chinese, or worked out their contracts and then moved on into farms and businesses of their own.

That is one of the biggest differences between what happened on the mainland and what happened in Hawaii. For Chinese-Americans on the mainland, the whole process of moving out on their own was stopped by the anti-Chinese hysteria and discriminatory laws of the time. In Hawaii, it was possible for Chinese immigrants to work out peaceably the dream of freedom and financial independence that brought so many immigrants of all races and peoples to America.

A Short-lived Bachelor Society

Families also developed very differently in Hawaii, in spite of some similar conditions. As on the mainland, almost all of the Chinese who came to work on the plantations were single men (although the merchant and skilled workers' groups had a far greater proportion of Chinese women than on the mainland). Discrimination on the mainland forced the development of a long-term bachelor society, with families broken up for decades, and the growth of a large prostitution industry in the Chinese-American community.

But in Hawaii, it was very different. There certainly were Chinese prostitutes, as well as criminals who imported and managed them. But, from the start, many Chinese men married Hawaiian women and started families. Later, as many Chinese-Hawaiians established their own businesses, many Chinese wives and children came to Hawaii from China, often sooner than on the mainland. The result was the development of a far healthier, stronger Chinese-Hawaiian community, with a much greater proportion of native-born Chinese-Hawaiian-Americans in that community.

Moving On

Even as early as the 1880s, when mainland Chinese-Americans were being forced off the land and sea and out of the mines, Chinese-Hawaiians were moving off the plantations in large numbers and into better occupations. By 1902, only 4,000 of the immigrants were left on the sugar plantations.

Many of the Chinese-Hawaiians went directly into the rice-growing industry, while others went from sugar to rice when their labor contracts had been completed. Some worked for wages growing rice, but many worked on some kind of profit-sharing arrangement, as partners or for some other kind of incentive. Many others went on their own as farmers, growing such cash-yielding crops as bananas, coffee, pineapples, potatoes, taros, and vegetables and fruits for local markets. Still others raised and sold cattle, mules, horses, chickens, pigs, ducks, and eggs. Some became fishers, catching everything from whales and sharks to eels, lobsters,

crabs, and mullet. No one was removed from the land or the sea; they were free to pursue their occupations, first as Hawaiians and later as Americans.

As the economy of Hawaii developed, Chinese-Hawaiians also tended to move into far better-paying businesses, trades and professions. That has been normal wherever there have been overseas Chinese populations. Many of the earliest Chinese immigrants to Hawaii were businesspeople; and as Hawaii developed they went into many kinds of occupations. There were Chinese-Hawaiian peddlers in the countryside, small shopkeepers in every kind of retail business, moneylenders, medical practitioners, cooks, barbers, domestic workers, garment makers, jewelers, and skilled construction workers.

In later years the Chinese-Hawaiians became fully integrated into Hawaiian-American life. Large numbers of Chinese-Hawaiian-Americans moved into professional and white-collar jobs. By the 1930s there were also many teachers, journalists, bankers, interpreters, ministers, doctors, managers, and other professionals in Hawaii's Chinese-American community. By then Chinese-American women had also come to play an important role in Hawaii's work force. Many had moved into the professions, and especially into teaching. Today, Hawaii's Chinese-Americans are to be found largely in business and the professions, as well as in the mainstream of American life in Hawaii.

Anti-Chinese Movements

But wait; all was not sweetness and light for Hawaii's Chinese-Americans. The mainland experience was so much worse that it is easy to overlook some of the bitter anti-Chinese feeling and action that surfaced in Hawaii as Chinese immigrants began to arrive in large numbers in the 1870s and 1880s. Nor was Hawaii at all immune to the wave of anti-Chinese hysteria sweeping the West Coast in those times.

By 1883, Hawaii's Workingmen's Union had been formed. In program and approach, it was much like Dennis Kearney's anti-Chinese Workingmen's Party on the West Coast. Starting in 1887, the vote was taken away from Chinese-Hawaiians born outside Hawaii. This was one of many pieces of anti-Chinese legislation in those years. After annexation by the United States, the importation of Chinese laborers was stopped, and the Chinese exclusion laws of the United States were applied to Hawaii. Only in the 1950s and 1960s, with new immigration laws, did substantial numbers of Chinese immigrants again begin to arrive in Hawaii.

Honolulu's Chinatown was by far the largest Chinese-Hawaiian community. No mob ever threatened to burn it down, as they tried in San Francisco in 1877. But government action did burn it down during the bubonic plague epidemic of 1899-1900, as the health authorities tried to stop the spread of the disease by burning buildings that had held plague victims. Many Hawaiian-Chinese-Americans felt the action to have been unnecessary, and due to anti-Chinese prejudice.

Community Life

The life of the Chinese-American community in Hawaii was not exactly the same as that of the mainland community. But there were some similarities. Most of the people in both communities were from the same part of China, and were moving, as immigrants, into different but in some ways quite similar situations. Their organizations, political views, newspapers, and entertainments were therefore similar, especially because each community knew what the other was doing and thinking.

The same district and family associations could be found in Hawaii as on the mainland. And the same fraternal organizations, too, sometimes with their criminal elements running the same kinds of illegal activity. The district, family, and fraternal groups were extensions of existing Chinese organizations, both on the mainland and in Hawaii.

The United Chinese Society performed many of the same functions in Hawaii as the Six Companies did on the mainland. In some periods, the Society had a lot to do with running the Chinese-Hawaiian community, just like the Six Companies. That was particularly so in times of crisis and

Hiram Fong (standing third from left), the first Chinese-American senator, celebrated his Hawaiian background with a staged island feast for his Washington colleagues. (Copyright Washington Post; reprinted by permission of the D.C. Public Library)

when the community was defending itself against legal attacks. For example, the United Chinese Society took over refugee care activities after the Honolulu Chinatown fire of 1866, which destroyed the community. It also took over health care and food distribution during the cholera epidemic of 1895. And in the 1890s, when law after anti-Chinese law as passed by the Hawaiian government, it was the community's main legal defense organization.

9

A New Day

By 1911, the now-weak Manchu Empire in China was coming to an end. China's defeat by the English in the Opium War of 1839-1842 had begun over a century of wars, civil wars, and the tearing apart of Chinese society. The huge Taiping rebellion of the 1850s and 1860s greatly damaged the ability of the Manchus to rule China. The European countries took advantage of China's growing weakness, and took concession after concession out of China, further weakening the Manchus. Meanwhile, some Chinese began to be influenced by new ideas of freedom from the West. Many of them also began to believe that it was time for China to modernize its industries and whole society.

At the same time, there was a strong reaction in Manchu China against demands for modernization and against all foreign influences. With the quiet agreement of the Manchus, the nationwide Boxer Society in the late 1890s began attacking foreigners. By 1900, these attacks had become a full-scale war against foreigners. But the Europeans were too strong. European and American forces smashed the Chinese army, took Peking, and demanded huge new payments and concessions from the Manchus. After that, the country began to fall apart. Local Chinese military commanders, called *warlords*, took over large parts of the country.

Now the Manchus were very weak, and a new day was bound to come. New revolutionary movements began to form in China, looking toward the end of Manchu rule and the formation of a Chinese republic. The most important, and finally the most successful of these was the movement led by Sun Yat-sen, the founder of the Republic of China, who became to the people of China what George Washington is to the people of the United States. From 1894 until the success of the revolution in 1911, he led expedition after expedition into China to try to finish the Manchus. In the same period, he traveled the world, raising money and building support for the cause of Chinese freedom. He became the first president of the Chinese Republic on January 1, 1912.

But China's time of troubles was far from over. For the next 37 years, until 1949, there was war in China. Sun's party, the Kuomintang, fought

On the eve of the 1911 Chinese Revolution, these young children celebrating the Chinese New Year reflect a society caught between two cultures, the old and the new. (Library of Congress, Bain Collection)

the warlords, finally uniting China in 1928. Sun himself had died in 1925, and Chiang Kai-shek had become leader of the Republic of China. But Chiang and China's new Communist Party (which had supported the republic) split, and in 1927 the Chinese Civil War began. It lasted 22 years, until Communist victory in 1949.

And there was more. In 1931, while the Chinese Civil War was raging, the Japanese army took China's northern province of Manchuria. Then, in 1937, Japan invaded China itself, and took a good deal of the country. For a little while, Chiang and Mao Tse-tung (who had become leader of the Communists) fought the Japanese invaders together. But they soon returned to fighting each other, as well. So, for some years, there was a three-way war among Republicans, Communists, and Japanese in China.

In 1941, Japan bombed Pearl Harbor, and the United States joined China's fight against Japan as a part of World War II. During the war, Communist and Republican forces both fought against the Japanese, more than against each other. But as soon as the world war ended, the civil war broke out again. It ended only with the final Communist victory and the establishment of the People's Republic of China, on October 1, 1949. This is the present government of China.

Chiang Kai-shek and his supporters fled to the island of Taiwan (Formosa), off the Chinese coast. There they continued to maintain that they were the rightful rulers of China.

The revolution of 1911 and all that followed were of great importance to China and to Chinese ethnic communities all over the world. The revolution brought a new day to China—and the beginning of a new day to the Chinese-American communities in the United States and Hawaii, as well.

Long before the 1911 revolution, Sun Yat-sen had been a very special figure to Chinese-Americans. Like them, he was from Kwangtung. And the great revolutionary movement he led had its start in Kwangtung. The revolution itself had some of its greatest early successes in that same area, and the impact on Chinese-Americans was enormous.

Chinese-Americans played a large role in the preparation of the Chinese revolution. Sun Yat-sen's first revolutionary organization, the Revive China society, was formed in Honolulu, Hawaii, in 1894. Its membership was composed of people like Sun himself, Kwangtungese then living in Hawaii.

In 1904, Sun came to the mainland United States. He was held as an illegal alien, and nearly deported to China. There, he would have been executed. But he won admission to the United States, with the help of San Francisco's Chinese-Americans. He then enlisted the help of the powerful Triad Society, with its hundreds of years of anti-Manchu history. He toured the United States, together with Triad society leaders, using a traveling Cantonese opera troupe to bring in crowds that would stay to hear him speak. Sun spent many years leading armed revolts against the Manchus, and building organizations among overseas Chinese all over the world. By 1911, Sun and his co-workers had built a strong American organization, which sent large amounts of money to help the Chinese revolution.

Into the Mainstream

After the 1911 revolution, some Chinese-American immigrants went back to help Sun build a new, republican China. Most, however, stayed in the United States, and began to build a new Chinese-American community. Men cut off the detested Manchu queue and wore their hair American-style. Women, and especially young American-born women, began to move into the professions as equals. Men and women coming from China to America began to reflect the new, free, and far more equal society of the Chinese republic. A whole process of Americanization began to take place. Once started, it grew into the main movement in the Chinese-American community. People began to wear American-style clothes, learned to speak English well, and organized Boy Scout troops and Young Men's and Young Women's Christian Associations. In short, even while exclusion was still being practiced, Chinese-Americans began the process of moving into the mainstream of American life.

In these early decades of the 20th century, Chinese-Americans also began to move into the political life of the country. As more and more second-generation, American-born people began to grow up in the community, new, Americanized political organizations began to take shape. In 1895, California's Chinese-Americans formed the Native Sons of the Golden State. By 1905, this had developed into the Chinese-American Citizens Alliance, which soon became a substantial, national political action and education organization. It developed branches in many cities and built its own headquarters in San Francisco. Wherever there was a Chinese-American community, it built Chinese-American political strength. The alliance published a newspaper, *Chinese Times*, which was a strong, continuing voice for the new forces in the Chinese-American community. The development of such political action and educational groups is normal to all ethnic communities, as they move into the mainstream of American life. What was unusual about the Chinese-American experience was that the whole process had been delayed so long because of the anti-Chinese hysteria the early Chinese-Americans faced.

The early Chinese-American political organizations tended to sympathize mainly with the Republican Party. That is entirely understandable, for there were very strong anti-Chinese forces in the Democratic Party all during the 19th century and well into the 20th century. Indeed, it was only in the 1930s, when a major minorities and labor coalition was put together under Franklin Roosevelt's New Deal, that Chinese-Americans in any real numbers became Democrats. In 1932, the New York Chinese-American community turned decisively toward the Democrats, spurred by a strong, new Chinese-American Voting League. In the 1950s, a national Chinese-American Democratic Club was formed.

The Students

From the early 19th century, many young Chinese students had come to the United States. The small number who had arrived at Cornwall, Con-

In the years just before World War I, Chinese and other immigrants in cities like New York City moved into the American mainstream aided by education in the public schools. (Library of Congress)

necticut, to study between 1818 and 1825 were only the vanguard of what would later become thousands. All during the years of the main Chinese-American immigration, starting with Yung Wing in the 1850s, Chinese students had come to America. In the early years, most were missionary-sponsored, and drawn from the same classes and places as the immigrants were. But in the early 1900s, young people began to come to United States schools from all over China. They were part of a wave of Chinese who were spreading out to study throughout the world, as China began to modernize. Tens of thousands of Chinese students went abroad. The largest numbers went to Japan, but thousands went to Great Britain, France, Germany, and the United States. The great majority of the students were sent on scholarships, though some were supported by their families, and then went home to China after finishing their studies.

Among those who came to study in the United States was Charles Soong, who began his American college education at Trinity College, North Carolina, in 1880, and graduated from Vanderbilt University. He founded the most prominent of Chinese Republic families. He and his son-in-law, H.H. Kung, worked for the 1911 revolution with Sun Yat-sen, and later became the most powerful financiers in China. His second daughter, Ching-ling, went to Wesleyan College in Georgia. Back in China, she married Sun Yat-sen. Later, Madame Sun Yat-sen was a vice chairman of the People's Republic of China. His third daughter, May-ling, also went to Wesleyan. She married Chiang Kai-shek, who ruled China from the late 1920s to 1949. As Madame Chiang Kai-shek, she was one of the best known women of her time. One of Soong's sons, Tse-Ven, was educated at Harvard and later became a prime minister of China.

Though the Soongs were the most prominent, they were certainly not the only American-educated Chinese. By the late 1930s, most of the leading people in Chiang Kai-shek's Republic of China were American-educated. One very important reason for this was that President Theodore Roosevelt had made a key move in United States-China relations back in the early 1900s. In 1900, the Chinese Boxer movement, with the consent of the Manchus, attacked foreigners in China, besieging them in Peking, the Chinese capital. Eventually, the siege was lifted by large forces of foreign troops, among them Japanese and Americans, and the forces of several European powers. Afterward, the defeated Manchus were forced to pay large penalties to many countries. Uniquely, Theodore Roosevelt directed that much of the American share of these penalty payments be used to set up American-Chinese scholarship funds and to build China's

Even in the desperately hard times of the Depression, Chinese-Americans continued to make a living in small towns and cities around the country, as here in Leland, Mississippi, in 1939. (By Marion Post Wolcott, U.S. Department of Agriculture, Farm Security Administration; Library of Congress)

Tsing Hua University. The university was built in 1911, and prepared thousands of Chinese students for American study.

Another Revolution

In 1949, Chinese Communist forces finally won China from Chiang Kai-shek's Kuomintang, setting up the People's Republic of China. At that time, there were thousands of Chinese students in American colleges and universities, as well as many Chinese scientists, teachers, businesspeople, and others in the United States. Most of these had ties to the defeated government, and felt that they could not safely return to China. About 4,000 Chinese students and about 1,000 other Chinese took refuge in the United States. Some were harassed by the United States government, then in the midst of the "red scare" promoted by Senator Joseph McCarthy and others. But the great majority were given the refuge they wanted. Most eventually decided to stay on and build new lives in the United States. But not all. Some went to the island of Taiwan, where Chiang Kai-shek's defeated government took refuge. Others went to Chinese communities outside China, in such places as Hong Kong and Singapore. A small number also eventually went home to China—though some skilled Chinese scientists and technicians had to win permission from a reluctant American government, which did not want their skills to serve the Chinese Communists.

Those who stayed in the United States introduced a whole new element into the Chinese-American community. These students, scientists, other intellectuals, and businesspeople were some of the best-educated and most highly skilled people in China. They were not many—only about 5,000 people added to the Chinese-American community then about 150,000 strong—but they made an enormous difference. For Americans—and even bigoted Americans, of whom many remained—it was impossible to see these new Chinese-Americans as anything but highly visible, enormous achievers. Before, Chinese-Americans could point with pride to such people as the internationally acclaimed actress Anna May Wong, the great cinematographer James Wong Howe, and the fine artist, Dong Kingman. Now these were joined by such people as Nobel Prize-winning physicists Chen-ning Yang and Tsung-dao Lee, world renowned architect I.M. Pei, and scores of other prominent new Chinese-Americans.

These new Chinese-American immigrants immediately moved into the mainstream of American life. They tended to live in high-income mixed communities, rather than in ethnic communities, though many of them also became active in Chinese studies. In this, they were like second- and third-generation Chinese-Americans—the children and grandchildren of immigrants—and like some of the new immigrants who would come in later years.

America changes. That is the secret of much of its vigor and ability to grow as the world changes. During World War II, when America was allied with China against Fascism, the old anti-Chinese bigotries and the old exclusionary policies just would not do. After the war, even though immigration was still greatly restricted, there began a small, steady flow of Chinese wives and children, joining their American husbands. Some of these were Chinese families being reunited, but others were war wives joining their soldier, sailor, and marine husbands. Then, in 1952, the still-discriminatory immigration laws were changed to make it much easier for Chinese women to join their Chinese-American husbands.

Chinese-American I.M. Pei, shown here with his wife at a 1980 gallery opening, is one of the most respected architects of the 20th century. (Copyright Washington Post; *reprinted by permission of the D.C. Public Library)*

As a result, the old Chinatown communities, with single men clustered together around the district and family associations, and around the tongs, began to become history. Instead, there emerged a more widespread pattern of tightly knit Chinese-American families.

In this era of great changes both in China and in the Chinese-American community, the traditional Chinese-American family also changed. The old traditions had called for arranged marriages, the complete authority of the men over the women in the family, and the unquestioned authority of the old over the young in the family. The early 20th century saw the beginning of the end of such practices, though they would still have great weight into the mid-20th century. On the one hand, the American-born children of early Chinese immigrants were more and more inclined to behave like the other Americans around them, which meant such things as marrying for love and limiting family size. On the other hand, the immigrants who came after the American barriers began to fall were coming from a more modern China.

The new families were American families, with Chinese and American roots. They were families that shared community concerns. Such ordinary local matters as school budgets, Little League, and garbage collection gradually became more important in day-to-day life than the affairs of an association. On some Sundays, the whole family might go into the nearest big Chinese-American community for many kinds of activity, just as Hungarians might go into New York's Yorkville or Italians into New York's Little Italy. But that was a matter of long-term shared history, and a voluntary choice, rather than a need to huddle together as foreigners in an alien, hostile land.

Changing Occupations

As the second generation grew up and moved out into the world of work, Chinese-Americans pursued many new occupations. Chinese immigrants may earlier have been driven from the land, sea, and mines into laundries, restaurants, and domestic work, but their children moved out into the American mainstream. This generation was educated in American schools, for the whole range of careers open to all American citizens. There was certainly still a great deal of discrimination. A young Chinese-American growing up in the early years of this century could not really look forward to becoming president of the United States, any more than a young Black or Native American could in those years. But by mid-century she or he could look forward to becoming a teacher, scientist, doctor, engineer, pharmacist, manager, politician, or any of the other main kinds of professional and businesspeople on the American scene. In our lifetime, there may very well be a Chinese-American president.

There are still very few Chinese-American farmers, however. Once driven from the land, they never returned. This is, indeed, a strange and sad circumstance in Chinese-American history—for this is one of humanity's great farming peoples.

For most native-born Chinese-Americans, as well as for the stranded students and their families, the process of Americanization has meant moving out into the American middle class. But this is not true for all. Many Chinese-Americans, especially the elderly and those who are new immigrants, are poor and greatly disadvantaged. Immigration continues,

In the years after World War II, many Chinese women moved into the work force alongside men, as at this Long Island printing plant that produced documents for the United Nations (National Archives)

and with it all the problems and injustices that have come with the immigration of many other peoples into the United States. Now, however, the processes of Americanization and upward economic movement also continue, without the enormous strains and injustices caused by the terrible bigotry and exclusion of the early years.

Chinese-American Women

Whether born in America or China, Chinese-American women today emerge more and more as equals. That is so in China, as well as in the United States, although there is a long way to go before complete equality will be achieved in either country. There are certainly Chinese-American women artists, writers, doctors, scientists, political figures, and managers, just as there are women of all ethnic backgrounds moving up in American society today. But Chinese-American women continue to experience discrimination in American society, both as Chinese-Americans and as women.

Still, the situation is much improved. Chinese-American women are no longer expected to stay at home and live almost entirely with and for their own families. Anna May Wong, as an outstanding achiever in the arts, is no longer an exception. Now she has been joined by such highly skilled and nationally recognized Chinese-American women novelists as Maxine Kingston and Jade Snow Wong, whose work has done so much to help Chinese-Americans free themselves from the old restrictions. These novelists, and others like them, have a double role in the Chinese-American community. As celebrities, they function as encouraging role models for others on their way up. At the same time, the subject matter of their works, which are about Chinese-Americans, and especially about Chinese-American women, helps others to see the many paths to personal freedom all the more clearly.

There are also women—and men—who celebrate the Chinese-American heritage. One such is Tisa Chang, whose Pan Asian Repertory Company in New York City has been greatly successful in bringing an awareness of many of the cultures of East Asia to the United States.

Chinese women have moved as equals and leaders into many highly visible portions of American life. For example, Tiffany Chin is a world-famous skater, and Connie Chung is a nationally known news commentator. Behind these leaders will come scores, hundreds, and eventually thousands of Chinese-American women, successfully reaching for the freedom and equality that is their American birthright.

Connie Chung, NBC news anchor shown here in 1977, is a model of the highly successful and articulate Chinese-American woman of the late 20th century. (Copyright Washington Post; *reprinted by permission of the D.C. Public Library)*

Recent Chinese Immigrants

Easing of immigration policies has continued. Starting in 1962, President John F. Kennedy used existing immigration laws to admit 15,000 Chinese on a temporary basis. Most of these stayed to become Americans. Then, in 1965, and again in 1970 and 1976, substantially new immigration laws replaced the old restrictive laws of the 1920s; these made it possible for an average of over 20,000 Chinese each year to come to the United States. Most came as immigrants, with the rest coming under several other classifications, but really as immigrants, too.

Many came with their children. Most had children after they settled in the United States. By now, many of their children have had children of their own. The result of it all was that 150,000 Chinese-Americans in 1950 became 237,000 in 1960, 435,000 in 1970, 860,000 in 1980, and at least a million today. This is a very small percentage of the total population of the United States, but a large number of new immigrants for so small an ethnic group to absorb in such a short time.

Although most of the new immigrants came through Hong Kong, they were in fact from all over China. Many of them were skilled and educated people who were able to make their way very quickly in America. A good many were of much the same background as the stranded students of the early 1950s; they were well-educated people who had left China due to the change of government in 1949.

At the same time, many of the new arrivals were poor immigrants who spoke only Chinese. They had little or no money, and few of the skills they might need to make their way in their new country. Normal enough—and the history of many people, in all the ethnic groups, who have come to America. These new immigrants tended to crowd into the Chinese-American communities of San Francisco, New York, Los Angeles, Chicago, Seattle, and a dozen other cities. And, as has been true of many ethnic groups upon starting the long process of an American immigrant experience, there have been some problems.

Some of the problems have been political. New immigrant groups tend for some time to reflect the political issues in their native lands. For the new Chinese-Americans, this has meant a pull between those who favor the People's Republic of China and those who prefer the Republic of China government based in Taiwan. Many of the leading people and organizations in the older Chinese-American community have continued to support the Taiwan government as the legal government of China. They were joined by many of the new immigrants, themselves refugees from the government of the People's Republic of China. But many of the new immigrants, and some people in the older Chinese-American community, sympathized with the new Chinese Communist government. During the McCarthy period, and somewhat beyond, this disagreement was greatly complicated by the American government's campaign against supporters of the Communist government. Loyalty oaths and deportation proceedings created great scars in the Chinese-American community, many of which have not yet healed.

Many Chinese-Americans retain a strong interest in Chinese politics; these young children in the Washington, D.C., Chinatown are celebrating the 63rd anniversary of the 1911 Chinese Revolution. (Copyright Washington Post; reprinted by permission of the D.C. Public Library)

Just five years after she had arrived in America, Jeannie Chen was a sophomore in college and worked as supervisor at a fast food restaurant, where she hosted these visiting Chinese scholars. (Copyright Washington Post; reprinted by permission of the D.C. Public Library)

Some of the problems have been economic. Like unskilled people in other immigrant groups, poor Chinese immigrants have in modern times been victimized by some employers, who have set up substandard, low-wage, unsafe operations in and near the Chinese-American communities. In San Francisco and New York, hundreds of garment industry sweatshops are in operation. These employ thousands of new Chinese-Americans, most of them women, in conditions as bad as those that existed in the sweatshops of almost a century ago. Union organization proceeds slowly, and in many places corrupt local officials make it hard to enforce existing health and safety laws. Low wages also make it much harder to move out of substandard housing into decent housing. But most of these difficulties will pass, as honest officials enforce the laws and workers continue to organize themselves. The question of housing will be by far the most difficult to solve. It is hard for working people to find decent housing in the cities at a reasonable price.

The economic problems are particularly difficult for both young and old in the center-city Chinese-American communities. In the Chinatowns of today's San Francisco and New York, there are thousands of older people with little money, trapped in poverty. They are forced to rely on social services to help them survive. In the same places, there are thousands of young people, many of them young Chinese-American immigrant teenagers, trapped in a vicious circle of unemployment, school dropout, poverty, despair, and gang activity. In such conditions, Chinese-American youth gangs flourish, just as they have flourished in other such immigrant communities. In these conditions, the secret societies can flourish again, running illegal activities out of Macao and Hong Kong into the American cities, much as they did a century ago.

But although much publicity is given to gang killings in the Chinatowns and drug dealing out of Macao and Hong Kong into the United States, these are not the main trends in the Chinese-American community. Movies about Chinatown, full of drugs, murder, and sex, make money for their producers, but they have very little to do with what is happening in the Chinese-American community. After all, some television stations are still making money by showing old Charlie Chan and Fu Manchu movies, with all their lies about wily Orientals and their sinister vices.

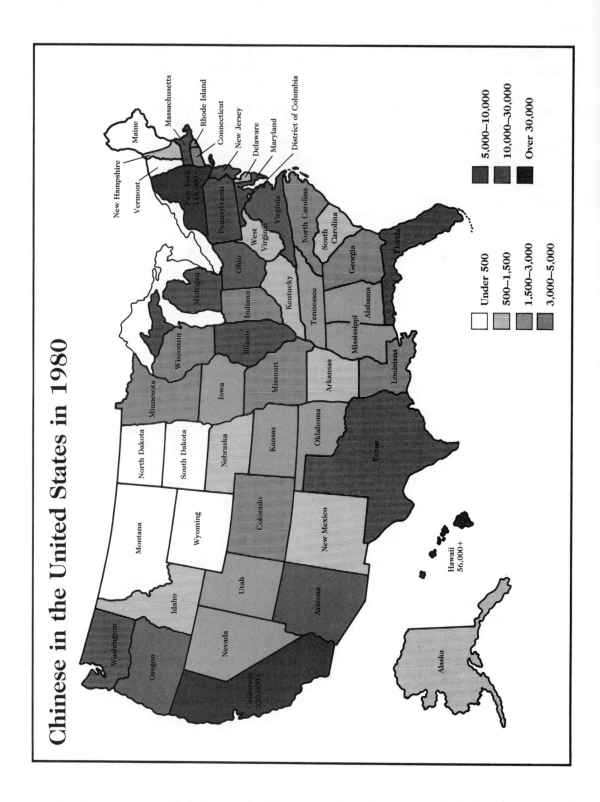

Chinese in the United States in 1980

New Hampshire
Vermont
Maine
Massachusetts
Rhode Island
Connecticut
New Jersey
Delaware
Maryland
District of Columbia

New York
145,000+
Pennsylvania
Ohio
West Virginia
Virginia
North Carolina
South Carolina
Georgia
Florida

Michigan
Wisconsin
Indiana
Kentucky
Tennessee
Alabama
Mississippi
Louisiana

Minnesota
Iowa
Illinois
Missouri
Arkansas
Oklahoma
Texas

North Dakota
South Dakota
Nebraska
Kansas
Colorado
New Mexico

Montana
Wyoming
Idaho
Utah
Arizona

Washington
Oregon
Nevada
California
320,000+

Hawaii
56,000+

Alaska

Under 500
500–1,500
1,500–3,000
3,000–5,000
5,000–10,000
10,000–30,000
Over 30,000

Moving On

The truth is that the vast majority of Chinese-American teenagers are excellent students, who are moving ahead to pursue first-class careers in America. As a result, today's and tomorrow's Chinese-American heroes are not likely to be gangsters, but rather doctors, performing artists, scientists, a governor or two, and perhaps in our lifetime that Chinese-American president.

The new Chinese-Americans are moving up in American society in great numbers. Many of them move into American society at a high level to start with. Many who have started out poor in "Chinatown" are already moving up and out into the larger American world.

One million and more Chinese-Americans are now freely mixing and merging their old and great heritage with the heritages of all Americans. The names of the leading people—physicists Chen-ning Yang and Tsung-dao Lee; novelist Maxine Hong Kingston, Senator Hiram Fong, skater Tiffany Chin, astronaut Taylor Wang, Dr. Katherine Hsu, financier Gerald Tsai, director Tisa Chang, broadcaster Connie Chung, and a hundred more—read like a Chinese-American *Who's Who*. But the leaders are also models for the tens and hundreds of thousands of others who come on behind them. They pave the way, much to their enduring honor, as do all the other leaders of the ethnic strains in the marvelous American mosaic. Now, Chinese-Americans have taken their place, and America is all the better for it.

Suggestions for Further Reading

Barth, Gunther P. *Bitter Strength: A History of the Chinese in the United States, 1850-1870*. Cambridge, Massachusetts: Harvard University Press, 1964.

Char, Tin-Yuke. *The Sandalwood Mountains*. Honolulu: University of Hawaii Press, 1975.

Chen, Jack. *The Chinese of America*. San Francisco: Harper & Row, 1980.

Cheng-tsu Wu. *Chink: Evidence of the Anti-Chinese Prejudice Pervading Our Country*. New York: World, 1972.

Chinese Historical Society of America. *The Life, Influence and the Role of the Chinese in the United States, 1776-1960*. San Francisco: The Chinese Historical Society of America, 1976.

Chu, Daniel and Samuel. *Passage to the Golden Gate: A History of the Chinese in America to 1910*. Garden City, New York: Doubleday, 1967.

Coolidge, Mary R. *Chinese Immigration*. New York: Henry Holt, 1909; reprint 1969.

Dicker, Laverne Mao. *The Chinese in San Francisco: A Pictorial History*. New York: Dover, 1979.

Fairbank, John K., Edwin O. Reischauer, and Albert M. Craig. *East Asia: The Modern Transformation*. Boston: Houghton Mifflin, 1965. Volume Two of "A History of East Asian Civilization"; see Reischauer.

Franck, Irene M., and David M. Brownstone. *The Silk Road*. New York: Facts On File, 1986.

————. *To the Ends of the Earth*. New York: Facts On File, 1984.

Gernet, Jacques. *A History of Chinese Civilization*. Cambridge: Cambridge University Press, 1982. Translated by J.R. Foster.

Glick, Clarence E. *Sojourners & Settlers: Chinese Migrants in Hawaii*. Honolulu: University of Hawaii Press, 1980.

Herrman, Albert. *An Historical Atlas of China*. Edinburgh: Edinburgh University Press, 1966.

Hoexter, Corinne K. *From Canton to California: The Epic of Chinese Immigration*. New York: Four Winds Press, 1976.

Hsu, Francis L. *The Challenge of the American Dream: The Chinese in the United States*. Belmont, California: Wadsworth, 1972. Part of the "Minorities in American Life" series.

Kingston, Maxine Hong. *China Men*. New York: Knopf, 1980

Latourette, Kenneth Scott. *The Chinese: Their History and Culture*. New York: Macmillan, 1967.

Lee, Rose Hum. *The Chinese in the United States of America*. Hong Kong: Hong Kong University Press, 1960.

Lyman, Stanford M. *Chinese Americans*. New York: Random House, 1974. Part of the "Rose Series: Ethnic Groups in Comparative Perspective."

Mark, Diane Mei Lin, and Ginger Chih. *A Place Called Chinese America*. Dubuque, Iowa: Kendall-Hunt, 1982.

McCunn, Ruthanne Lum. *An Illustrated History of the Chinese in America*. San Francisco: Design Enterprises of San Francisco, 1979.

Meltzer, Milton. *The Chinese Americans*. New York: Crowell, 1980.

Miller, Stuart C. *The Unwelcome Immigrant: The American Image of the Chinese, 1785-1882*. Berkeley: University of California Press, 1969.

Miller, Wayne Charles. *A Comprehensive Bibliography for the Study of American Minorities*, two vols. New York: New York University Press, 1976.

Reischauer, Edwin O., and John K. Fairbank. *East Asia: The Great Tradition*. Boston: Houghton Mifflin, 1960. Volume One of "A History of East Asian Civilization"; see Fairbank.

Sih, Paul K.T. and Leonard B. Allen, eds. *The Chinese in America*. New York: St. John's University Press, 1976.

Steiner, Stan. *Fusang, the Chinese Who Built America*. New York: Harper & Row, 1980.

Sung, Betty Lee. *Mountain of Gold: The Story of the Chinese in America*. New York: Macmillan, 1967.

Thernstrom, Stephan, ed. *Harvard Encyclopedia of American Ethnic Groups*. Cambridge, Massachusetts: Harvard University Press (Belknap), 1980.

Tsai, Shih-Shan H. *China & the Overseas Chinese in the United States: 1868-1911*. Fayetteville: University of Arkansas Press, 1983.

————. *The Chinese Experience of America*. Indianapolis: Indiana University Press, 1986.

Tung, W.L. *The Chinese in America 1820-1973: A Chronology and Fact Book*. Dobbs Ferry, New York: Oceana, 1974.

Yung Wing. *My Life in China and America*. New York: Henry Holt, 1909.

Index